Rochester History

FALL 2025

Rochester History

*A publication of the Rochester Public Library
in partnership with Rochester Institute of Technology*

Volume 83, Issue 1

Contents

As the new director of the Rochester Public Library and the Monroe County Library System, I continue to discover the depth and richness of this remarkable city and its surrounding communities each day. Rochester's cultural, economic, and social history offers a wealth of unexpected insights and compelling narratives—stories that not only ignite our imagination but also provide critical context for understanding the present. Thanks to the work of our City Historians, past and present, we are fortunate to have access to a dynamic historical record that deepens our collective understanding of Rochester. This issue of *Rochester History* highlights the legacy of City Historian Blake McKelvey, whose scholarship continues to shape both our local knowledge and the broader field of urban historical studies.

At a time when the methods of recording and interpreting history are rapidly evolving, it is more vital than ever to support the role of the City Historian and to ensure equitable public access to historical resources. The Rochester Public Library remains deeply committed to preserving and disseminating our shared history, ensuring that future generations have the opportunity to explore and learn from it. ∎

Emily Clasper
Director, Rochester Public Library and the Monroe County Library System

Dear reader,

In this issue, we are pleased to offer you a retrospective consideration of the work and career of former City Historian Blake McKelvey.

The year 2025 marks the eightieth anniversary of the publication of McKelvey's *Rochester: The Water-Power City, 1812–1854*, the first book in what would be a four-volume exploration of Rochester's journey from settlement to technological powerhouse. Through his research and writing, McKelvey helped to define the field of urban history in the United States, as well as the role of a city historian.

We have gathered multiple voices to help us assess the legacy of McKelvey and his work. Nancy Hewitt provides us with an overview of this anniversary moment. Our current city historian, Christine L. Ridarsky, reflects on the life and career of one of her predecessors. Michael Brown offers a consideration of McKelvey's career as a historian. Brown invites us to think through the implications of McKelvey's work. What does it mean to write a biography—not of a person, but of a city? Finally, Christine Keiner draws our attention to the water in the water-power city. While McKelvey is not generally considered an environmental historian, Keiner mounts a convincing case that McKelvey was ahead of his time in emphasizing nature's role in Rochester's rise.

Our reviews in this issue move us from McKelvey's nineteenth-century origin story into Rochester's twentieth-century history. Sarah Thompson explores the legacy of Rochester's artistic past, reviewing the Memorial Art Gallery's exhibit and book about the work of artists

M. Louise Stowell and Harvey Ellis at the turn of the twentieth century. We continue the consideration of Rochester's place in the Arts and Crafts movement with Aspen Golann's review of Bruce Austin's *A Symbiotic Partnership: Marrying Commerce to Education at Gustav Stickley's 1903 Arts & Crafts Exhibitions*.

Finally, Hon. Richard Dollinger, ret., reviews Bruce W. Dearstyne's *The Crucible of Public Policy: New York Courts In the Progressive Era*. In considering this work of legal history, Dollinger draws our attention to Rochester's part in shaping the right to privacy, in a case that centered around the question of the fair use of images captured by a new technology—the Kodak camera.

Christine L. Ridarsky and Rebecca Edwards
Editors

Rochester as water-power city and as image city. We hope you enjoy this panoramic view of Rochester history!

As a final note, we want to acknowledge Bruce A. Austin, who passed away in March. From 2020 to 2022, he was engaged in discussions with the College of Liberal Arts, the Provost, and the Rochester Public Library on involving RIT Press in the publication of *Rochester History*, a partnership that launched in spring of 2023. Austin stepped down as the director of RIT Press at the end of 2022, but he had set the foundation for this collaboration that has earned two prestigious grants, as well as a PROSE Award for Best New Journal in Humanities and Social Sciences. He will be missed. ◼

Introduction
A Forum on Blake McKelvey

Nancy A. Hewitt

For many Rochesterians fifty years old and older, Blake McKelvey is Rochester history. After receiving his PhD in history from Harvard University in 1933, he worked as a researcher for a multivolume history of Chicago and served as an editorial assistant for the Encyclopedia Britannica. Three years later, McKelvey was hired by Dexter Perkins as Rochester's new assistant city historian and was promoted to city historian on Perkins's retirement. Although McKelvey officially retired in 1973, he continued writing about, lecturing on, and documenting the history of the city until his death at age 97 in 2000.

Over the course of his career, McKelvey published twenty-five books, most of them chronicling Rochester's development from its founding in 1812 through 1961. In addition to providing deeply researched books, McKelvey also edited ten volumes of the Rochester Historical Society's publications. In 1939, he founded, edited, and, in the early years, wrote many of the articles in the then-quarterly journal *Rochester History*, which was published by the Rochester Public Library.

His influence reached well beyond his adopted hometown, however. McKelvey was a pioneer in the field of urban history and a founder of the Urban History Group within the American Historical Association, the largest organization of professional historians in the United States. McKelvey also gave dozens of radio talks and public lectures and taught at the University of Rochester, the University of Michigan, and Sir George William University (now Concordia University) in Montreal.

This forum focuses on McKelvey's earliest book-length study, *Rochester, The Water-Power City, 1812–1854*, published by Harvard University Press in 1945. The three contributors to this forum wield their expertise in urban history, public history, and science and technology to offer critical assessments of McKelvey's now-classic work. Their distinct perspectives illustrate the significance of his analysis while also noting issues and developments that he, and most historians of his era, failed to consider.

Christine L. Ridarsky, the current Rochester city historian, provides critical insights into the ways in which McKelvey shaped and expanded that position. She notes the crucial "Historian's Law" passed by the New York State Legislature in 1919, which required every municipality to appoint a historian to promote the preservation of government records, encourage historical societies and libraries to collect and preserve personal and organizational papers, and research and publish articles and books that would enhance public knowledge and appreciation of its community's history. Ridarsky traces the implementation of this mandate in Rochester from the city's appointment of its first city historian in 1921 and McKelvey's hiring as a full-time assistant historian in 1936 through his retirement. Inspired by his experiences at the Henry Street Settlement as a college student in 1924, McKelvey switched from his pre-med program to philosophy and then history. Influenced by Arthur Schlesinger while a graduate student at Harvard, McKelvey was swept up in the first wave of scholars studying the everyday lives and experiences of ordinary people. In 1948, McKelvey took over Perkins's position as city historian. Municipal funds supported his work, which inspired McKelvey to craft a groundbreaking four-volume "city biography." It was, Ridarsky argues, "the most complete history of any city in the U.S."[1] Although based on extensive research, the volumes were intended not for academics but for "the Citizens of Rochester."[2] He would be proud to know that vast numbers of city residents have taken advantage of his work to gain a deep understanding of Rochester's rich history.

Michael Brown, an associate professor of history at the Rochester Institute of Technology (RIT), captures the innovative vision McKelvey brought to his research, as well as the larger context in which he worked. Influenced by the generation of Progressive historians who preceded him, McKelvey was a leading figure in the development of the field of urban history and in the professionalization of local history. Brown notes that McKelvey envisioned his study of Rochester as offering a "complete" history of the city and as a "biography" that would have "civic value" for its readers.

But what constitutes a complete history, and which aspects of the past offer civic value? By the 1960s, urban historians were writing largely for a scholarly audience and were often critical of earlier works that lacked "analytical heft." McKelvey likely was not bothered by such criticisms since he claimed that his "first obligation is to the citizens of Rochester" and that "he intended his history to have some public benefit." In that effort, he highlighted individual actions that shaped the city's development in order to "enliven citizens' sense of their own creative powers."

Yet Brown notes that while urban historians of McKelvey's generation sought to provide "the life history of a community" and to pay attention to the "common man," they still paid far more attention to politics, business, and technological developments and to the actions of native-born white male residents than to women, immigrants, or African Americans. In the last of his four volumes on Rochester history, McKelvey did note "the ugly fact of racial segregation" in the city. Yet, as Brown notes, he failed to use the city's Black newspapers "to furnish a dissenting perspective on residential segregation and housing discrimination." Indeed, McKelvey rarely notes the presence of African Americans. He briefly mentions the African Methodist Episcopal Church and Frederick Douglass but does not recognize the importance of Black churches in the city, the strength of the antislavery movement, and Black Rochesterians' role in the Underground Railroad, nor the interracial work of the Western New York Anti-Slavery Society, headquartered in Rochester.

Nor would a reader of his book realize that Black men and white and Black women organized a stunning array of other benevolent and reform societies in the city between 1822 and 1961. McKelvey does mention the early work of the Rochester Female Charitable Society and the Rochester Orphan Asylum in passing, but he fails to note the importance of their work or that of the other institutions and organizations founded by women residents in this period and later. Fortunately, McKelvey's work has inspired younger scholars to expand upon his studies to provide a more complete history of the city.[3]

Christine Keiner, a professor of science, technology, and society at RIT, highlights another important aspect of McKelvey's work by analyzing environmental themes in *The Water-Power City*. This is a topic that has generally received little attention from historians of Rochester and Western New York, but McKelvey recognized its importance. Keiner notes, while highlighting the crucial role water played in urban development in the early nineteenth century, that humanity is now entering a new "age of water insecurity." Many cities were founded along fall lines, where rivers powered emerging industries. Focusing on "stories of urban nature-society relationships" in McKelvey's text, she explores the interplay and interdependence among Rochester, the Genesee River, and the Genesee Valley hinterlands. The opening chapter of *Water-Power City* analyzes the area's "Geologic and Human Background," and the second focuses on the early settlement as a "Bridgehead, a Milltown, or a Lake Port." McKelvey notes the presence of Native Americans in the region prior to white settlement yet describes members of the local Haudenosaunee nations "in the demeaning context of 'Local Antiquities and Clashing Empires.'" Yet they, like white settlers, were drawn to the region in part by its fertile lands and the ease of transportation along the Genesee River.

Anglo-American settlers were drawn by the Genesee River falls, which powered sawmills and grist mills and provided water routes to distant markets. McKelvey reports that only four years after its founding in 1812, Rochester had become "the principal grain market of western New York," a development ensured by the building of the Erie Canal through Rochester in the early 1820s. The canal cemented the city's critical role in larger commercial networks. Of course, such rapid development had unintended consequences, including the decimation of forests, the draining of swamps, and other changes to the existing landscape. Indeed, as "America's first boom town," Rochester suffered a variety of environmental crises, including floods, fires, and, beginning in 1832, several outbreaks of cholera. Keiner notes that when cholera returned in 1852, health officers finally opened an emergency hospital. They built "in the Negro quarter on High Street," placing the city's small African American community in jeopardy in order to secure benefits for white residents. Both disease and fire exposed the crucial links between "the urban environment, water infrastructure and human health."

By that time, Rochester had transitioned from the Flour City to the Flower City, which Keiner explains in environmental and economic terms. Western wheat had become cheaper than Genesee Valley wheat, requiring Rochesterians to find new products to sell. In the 1840s, immigrant farmers George Ellwanger and Patrick Barry began growing ornamental and fruit trees. Once again, the Erie Canal facilitated shipments to western markets, and Lake Ontario's moderating effect on the climate helped acclimate plants to "rigourous climates" better than its eastern competitors did. As water power was slowly replaced by coal in the 1840s and 1850s, local businesses made the transition but lost the competitive benefits long supplied by the Genesee Falls. McKelvey would tell that story in his second volume, *Rochester: The Flower City, 1855–1890*. ■

1. Christine Ridarsky, "History as a 'Municipal Enterprise,'" 18.
2. Ridarsky, "History," 27.
3. See Paul Johnson, *A Shopkeeper's Millennium: Society and Revivals in Rochester, New York, 1815-1837* (Hill and Wang, 1978); Nancy A. Hewitt, *Women's Activism and Social Change: Rochester, New York, 1822-1872* (Cornell University Press, 1984) and *Radical Friend: Amy Kirby Post and Her Activist Worlds* (University of North Carolina Press, 2018); Lou Buttino and Mark Hare, *The Remaking of a City: Rochester, New York, 1964-1984* (Kendall Hunt Publishing Co., 1984); Lauren Warren Hill, *Strike the Hammer: The Black Freedom Struggle in Rochester, New York, 1940-1970* (Cornell University Press, 2021); Justin Murphy, *Your Children Are Very Greatly in Danger* (Cornell University Press, 2022).

An undated portrait of former City Historian Blake McKelvey (1903–2000). *Courtesy of the Collection of the City Historian.*

History as a "Municipal Enterprise"

Christine L. Ridarsky, Rochester & Monroe County Historian

This year marks the eightieth anniversary of the publication of Blake F. McKelvey's *Rochester: The Water-Power City, 1812–1854*.[1] The book traces Rochester's development from frontier settlement through its establishment as a village, its growth into "America's first boom town," and its first twenty years as a city. The title reflects Rochester's location along the banks of the Genesee River and its early reliance on the power provided by a series of waterfalls, which turned the grindstones for early flour mills and later operated machinery in a variety of foundries and factories. The book was (and remains) remarkable for several reasons. For one, it was a deeply researched and detailed study of a single American city—produced in an era when scholars were only just beginning to explore the role and significance of cities in American history. When *Water-Power City* appeared in 1945, only a few other urban biographies were in print. The book was the first in what would become a four-volume series that detailed the growth and development of Rochester from its settlement by the first Europeans through 1961, giving Rochester the distinction of being one of, if not *the*, most well-documented mid-sized cities in the United States and establishing McKelvey as a pioneer in the then-nascent field of urban history.

Perhaps even more notable than the book's content or its place within the historiography was the source of support that made it possible. Blake McKelvey was serving as the City of Rochester's assistant historian when he produced *Water-Power City*. In other words, he was a government employee. City Historian Dexter Perkins highlighted this fact in the book's preface, and several reviewers found the unusual circumstances worthy of mention in their own descriptions of the work.[2] As Perkins wrote: "The present volume represents

Christine L. Ridarsky is the Rochester & Monroe County Historian and the coeditor of *Rochester History*.

if not a unique, at any rate a most striking, achievement, the preparation of a history of an important American city on the basis of careful research, exact scholarship, and expert judgment all provided for by municipal funds. . . . Yet more than that can be said. Not only preparation, but also the publication, of the work is a municipal enterprise."[3]

New York's Historian's Law

In calling attention to the unique positions that he and McKelvey held as historians working in local government, Perkins revealed the unusual commitment that New York State—and, by extension, the City of Rochester—had made to documenting, preserving, interpreting, and disseminating local history. This commitment came in the form of a law passed by the state legislature in 1919. Known as the "Historian's Law," and still in effect today, the legislation requires every municipality in New York to appoint a historian and outlines their responsibilities. These government-appointed historians are tasked with promoting the preservation of historically significant local government records; encouraging other organizations, such as libraries and historical societies, to collect and preserve nongovernmental historical records; and undertaking research—as well as encouraging others to do so—"in order to add to the knowledge, understanding and appreciation of the community's history." The law suggested that communities provide their historians with "space in a safe, vault or other fireproof structure" in which to safely store historical records. It also authorized municipalities to "appropriate, raise by tax and expend moneys for historical purposes," such as the preservation of "historical edifices, the erection of historical markers and monuments, the collection of war mementos . . . [and] the preparation and publication of local histories and records." Notably, the law did not require local governments to pay for their historians' services, stating that they "shall serve without compensation unless" their community "shall otherwise provide."[4]

Rochester was among the first municipalities in the state to implement the state's mandate, appointing Elmer Adler to the post in 1921. He served only six months before moving to New York City. He was replaced in June 1921 with attorney and history enthusiast Edward R. Foreman. Foreman was born in Lima, New York, in 1868 and moved to Rochester around 1888 to attend the University of Rochester. After graduating with a Bachelor of Philosophy in 1892 and being admitted to the state bar association in 1894, Foreman was hired as the assistant corporation counsel for the City of Rochester and held several positions in city government before being appointed the historian. Throughout his career, Foreman took an active interest in local history. By the time he became the city's official historian, he had served on the boards of the Genesee Country and New York State historical societies and was a five-time president of the Rochester Historical Society. Foreman's close association with the local historical society ensured that its work and that of the government-appointed historian would be closely aligned for decades.[5]

The first directive that New York State Historian James Sullivan gave the state's newly appointed historians was to compile a record of the men who had served in the recently concluded Great War. Foreman was one of the few to actually complete the project, resulting in the three-volume *World War Service Record of Rochester and Monroe County, New York*.[6] Upon publication of the last volume in 1930, *The Quarterly Journal of the New York Historical Association* declared, "No other city in the State has issued a work so complete, so inclusive, and so well edited."[7] Foreman also edited nine volumes of the Rochester Historical Society's Publication Series and five volumes of that organization's Centennial Series. This work built upon a foundation laid much earlier in newspaperman Henry O'Reilly's *Sketches of Rochester*. That book documented the city's settlement and development through its publication in 1838 and was described by Perkins as "invaluable to any student of Rochester history."[8] Thus, by the time Foreman died, Rochester had already done much to document its past.

With Foreman's unexpected passing from pneumonia in February 1936, Mayor Charles Stanton recruited Dexter Perkins as his replacement. At the time, the Boston-born and Harvard-educated Perkins was a respected professor at the University of Rochester and chair of its History Department. He made it clear that he had no intention of leaving his post at the university

Former City Historian Edward R. Foreman (sitting left) inspecting World War I service records with Mayor Clarence Van Zandt (sitting right), William Powers, and Robert Murphy on May 1, 1926. *From the Collection of the Rochester Public Library Local History & Genealogy Division.*

and, therefore, would be unable to commit to the government job full-time. He needed an assistant. Stanton agreed, so on June 2, 1936, Perkins accepted a part-time position as historian at an annual salary of $1,700 (the equivalent of about $39,000 today).[9] He quickly sought out and hired fellow Harvard graduate Blake McKelvey to serve as his full-time assistant. McKelvey's title belied the size of his role. "People have said that Blake McKelvey came to Rochester to assist Dexter Perkins," said J. Sheldon Fisher, noted Western New York collector and preserver of local heritage. "In fact, Blake McKelvey did all the work."[10]

A Budding Interest in Cities

Former City Historian Dexter Perkins on the River Campus of the University of Rochester ca. the 1930s. *Courtesy of University Archives Photograph Collection, UA915, Rare Books, Special Collections, and Preservation, River Campus Libraries, University of Rochester*

Blake McKelvey was born in Centralia, Pennsylvania, on June 10, 1903, to the Rev. Ellis Elmer McKelvey and Eva Rupert Faus.[11] As a Methodist minister, the elder McKelvey moved his family whenever he was called to service in a new location. This allowed Blake and his six siblings to experience life in an array of communities of various sizes, a fact he would later credit in part for his subsequent interest in cities. After graduating from high school in Williamsport, Pennsylvania, the young McKelvey enrolled in a pre-med program at Syracuse University, intending to become a medical missionary. He didn't take a single history course in his first three years. Then, in 1924, during his junior year, he had an opportunity to spend two months living and volunteering at the Henry Street Settlement in New York City.[12]

It was his first experience in a "big city." While there, he met frequently with students who were working at other settlements and "discussed the problems that a big city faced, many of them from [the] point of view of first-hand observation." He found it "fascinating." When he returned to Syracuse, he switched his major to philosophy, enrolled in two history classes, and took an interest in the problems of the off-campus city. One of his history professors recognized his potential and recommended that he pursue a master's degree. He moved on to Clark University in Worcester, Massachusetts. As he had in his final year at Syracuse, McKelvey enmeshed himself in studying that city's problems. He would do the same in Cambridge and Boston.[13]

Upon enrolling in Harvard's PhD program, McKelvey quickly connected with historian Arthur M. Schlesinger Sr., making it a point to attend the weekly teas the esteemed professor hosted for his graduate students.[14] At the time, there was no such field as "urban history." Schlesinger's approach was that of a social historian, a field he had begun to define in 1922 when he introduced the course "The Social and Cultural History of the United States" at the University of Iowa. A year later, he signed a contract with the Macmillan Company to coedit a multivolume *History of American Life*. The objective was to "free American history from its traditional servitude to party struggles, war and diplomacy and to show that it properly included all the varied interests of the people."[15] In retrospect, it seems natural that such an interest in the social and cultural forces in people's lives eventually would lead Schlesinger to look at cities.

His first serious foray into this work came in his 1933 book, *The Rise of the City, 1878–1898*. If that book invented the field of American urban history, as Andrea Tuttle Kornbluh has argued, Schlesinger's 1940 essay, "The City in American History," launched it.[16] Whereas historians working in the period preceding this had embraced Frederick Jackson Turner's "frontier thesis," which emphasized the significance of westward expansion on American political, social, and cultural development, Schlesinger challenged the assertion that US history could so easily be wrapped up in that expansionist view. Although Schlesinger didn't necessarily offer an alternative "urban interpretation" of the country's history, as Bruce M. Stave said, "he went far to shift emphasis away from Turner's frontier toward more urban themes. . . . He saw the city as a safety valve, as a place of social reform, and one that encouraged collective responsibility contrasted to frontier individualism. . . . Schlesinger claimed that the city, no less than the frontier, was a major force in shaping American civilization."[17]

It is difficult to overstate the influence that Schlesinger had on Blake McKelvey's career and, by extension, on Rochester. At Harvard, McKelvey's research hewed to Schlesinger's definition of social history. He produced a dissertation, subsequently published by the University of Chicago Press, on the history of

American prisons.[18] He acknowledged Schlesinger "for his thoughtful mentorship over a period of several years," not only in the methods of social history he applied to his thesis but also "in the broader study of urban history."[19] Those lessons would not be lost on McKelvey; he would make it his life's mission to advance the study of individual cities and, more generally, the processes of urbanization. He particularly took to heart Schlesinger's statement that "the American city has not yet been studied generically, nor do there exist any adequate social histories of particular cities."[20] This led McKelvey to embrace the genre of urban biography (also referred to as city biography), resulting in what is arguably the most complete history of any city in the US: his four-volume series on Rochester.[21]

Discovering Rochester

McKelvey graduated from Harvard in 1933, in the midst of the Great Depression, and moved back to Pennsylvania, where he was fortunate enough to be hired to survey historic documents as part of a New Deal–era program. The following year, he took a job as assistant to Bessie Pierce, who was working on the Rockefeller-funded History of Chicago project at the University of Chicago.[22] His experience in Chicago, combined with his work on the Pennsylvania survey, made him a perfect fit for the position working alongside Dexter Perkins in Rochester. As did his own aspirations: "Only three or four scholarly histories

An undated postcard image of the view from Cobb's Hill looking west.
From the Collection of the Rochester Public Library Local History & Genealogy Division.

of individual cities had yet appeared, and the prospect of contributing to the development of the new field of urban history had been a major attraction of the new job," McKelvey said.[23]

In June 1936, while McKelvey was in Rochester for an interview, Perkins drove him to the top of Cobbs Hill, where he could see the city stretched out across the horizon. "I can still recall my impression of Rochester as a tranquil home-owner's city spreading out under a green canopy with only a few office buildings, the Kodak Tower, and several chimneys and scattered steeples visible above the tree tops," he wrote thirty-seven years later, continuing with:

And that evening, as I strolled around downtown, I got a suggestive sense of its historic past. Crossing the Genesee River on Court Street Bridge, I had a good view of the old Erie Canal aqueduct, which then served as a subway crossing under Broad Street Bridge, thus spanning a century of urban and transportation history. On the west bank was the City Hall Annex housing the business branch of the Public Library in an aging brick structure with a massive chimney topped by a giant-sized statue of Mercury. Facing it on the east bank was the modern stone-faced structure of the new Rundel Memorial Library where, if I landed the job, my office would be located. Strolling north across the library's unfinished plaza and west onto Broad Street Bridge, I got a good view of

The newly completed Rundel Memorial building circa 1936. The statue of Mercury can be seen in the distance. *From the Collection of the Rochester Public Library Local History & Genealogy Division.*

two or three old stone mills bordering the river and of the backs of the three- and four-story brick buildings lining Main Street Bridge, the only replica of "Old London Bridge" in America. Curious about the history of these quaint structures, I strolled down Exchange Street to the Four Corners, where the massive Powers Block with its three Mansard roofs faced and overtopped the Elwood Building with gargoyles peering down from the four corners of its tower as if to warn passers-by of the historic mysteries that surrounded them. I was ready and eager to accept the job, when the offer arrived a week later.[24]

McKelvey started his work as the full-time assistant city historian on July 1 at an annual salary of $3,000 (the equivalent of about $69,366 today).[25] His first tasks were to complete the volume of the Rochester Historical Society's Publication Series that was in process when Foreman died and to compile an index of all of the volumes that had been published to that point. He would continue to edit one volume of the series each year until it ceased publication in 1948. In 1939, McKelvey began editing and writing for a new quarterly pamphlet series, *Rochester History*.[26] "This new publication had been inspired by a desire to reach a more general audience than that represented by the membership of the Rochester Historical Society," McKelvey recalled in 1973.[27] This desire to produce history aimed at the public would be a defining factor in McKelvey's work and that of his successors. The pamphlets, like McKelvey's subsequent work, were also a "municipal enterprise." With McKelvey's labor paid for by tax dollars and a private fund established to cover printing costs, the library was able to distribute *Rochester History* for free for many years.[28] As production costs increased, the library started charging a modest subscription fee, but it has always tried to keep that fee affordable to a general audience.

In the six years that preceded the publication of *Water-Power City*, McKelvey wrote ten essays (and edited ten others) for *Rochester History* on a wide array of early Rochester topics. These included the Phelps & Gorham Treaty, the city's first mills, civic and economic development, and, of course, the role of waterpower.[29] The effort that McKelvey put into both publication series laid the foundation for *Water-Power* City and the three volumes that would follow it.[30] "I don't know just when I conceived the plan of writing my own history of Rochester," he said, "but I was fascinated by the opportunity to study this city, and at some point during the first couple of years I determined to write a new, independent, one-man history of Rochester to supplement or

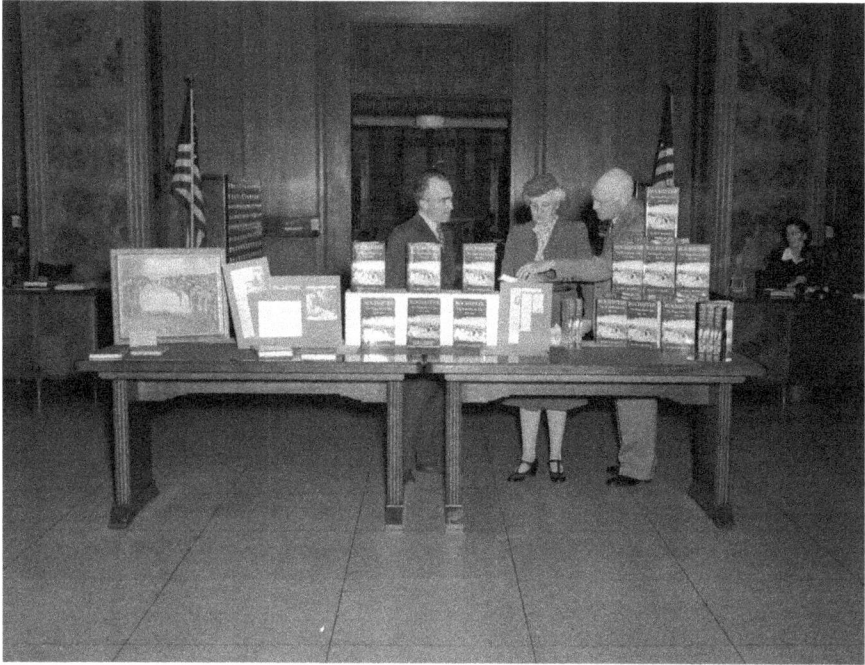

A circa 1954 display at the Rundel Memorial Library showcasing then-Assistant City Historian Blake McKelvey's *Rochester, the Water-Power City, 1812–1854. Courtesy of City of Rochester.*

replace the compilations that had been made by Foreman. I wanted to make a complete study."[31]

The Water-Power City

In preparation for his study of Rochester, McKelvey read Bessie Pierce's three-volume history of Chicago, Illinois; Constance Green's history of Holyoke, Massachusetts; Gerald Caper's volume on Memphis, Tennessee; and every other urban biography he could get his hands on. "I read them all," McKelvey said. "I especially wanted to know what was happening in other cities contemporary to the period of Rochester I was studying. I wanted to make anything I wrote as sound as possible, and I was looking at and developing a library of these other volumes and attending the American Historical Association meetings."[32] Each of these studies fell into the historical genre known as urban biography, which saw its heyday between 1930 and 1960. Urban biographers studied the growth and development of a city in much the same way that a biographer would do with a person.

McKelvey, like other urban biographers of the time, faced a challenge in having his work taken seriously. At the time, "local history" was considered to be the purview of amateurs, rather than of serious scholars.[33] Much of the criticism stemmed from the attention paid to individuals and the minute details of economic, political, religious, social, and cultural forces within the community under study, as well as the chronological arrangement upon which city biographers tended to rely. Urban biographies, by their very focus on a singular place, also tended to lack a deep analysis of the external factors that affected a city's development. *Water-Power City*, though generally well received, did not escape these criticisms. Dorothy Culp, for example, complimented McKelvey's ability to balance the "conflicting aims" of "satisfy[ing] those local groups who are interested in . . . minutiae" and "plac[ing] the story of his city in its broader regional and even national setting and show[ing] the interplay between local and larger forces and the effect of one upon the other." But she also noted that McKelvey's "involved style and an undue reverence for the chronological approach" obfuscated broader patterns.[34] Glyndon G. Van Deusen likewise found McKelvey's "devotion to detail a trifle wearisome."[35] Even a friend and colleague admitted that he found the first two or three chapters of *Water-Power City* "boring." "The first part of the book was really too much for me," Joe Norris wrote to McKelvey. "I got lost in a welter of towns, names of mill owners, and such ilk."[36]

In response to the criticism, McKelvey pointed out that his work was similar in nature to that of other urban biographers of the period. But, more importantly, he believed that his approach suited his audience:

> I think that the best way to respond to the criticism is to look at my interest in city history as compared to the majority of those interested in urban history. . . . It should be noted that my studies of Rochester particularly have not been written for scholars, but for the city. I've written them to be read by citizens in Rochester, and I have not been trying to prove a thesis; I've not been trying to demonstrate new insights into any subject. I've been trying to recreate the experiences of that community, growing into a modern city, and this is something that historians normally do chronologically. There is a question as to whether you take it topically, but even if you do take it topically you usually follow the topics chronologically. I decided early that there was a distinct advantage, within the periods that I took, in treating the multiple developments in their relationship at the time.[37]

Despite the criticism, urban biography continued to attract adherents. By the time McKelvey wrote his 1952 essay "American Urban History Today," the first two volumes of his history of Rochester were among forty urban biographies published since Schlesinger's call for more work on cities.[38] Interest in the field continued to grow, contributing to a rigorous debate about the definition of "urban history." Though less popular today, scholars continue to produce city biographies or variations thereof.[39]

Later, intellectuals identifying as "new urban historians" would find additional reasons to critique the work of McKelvey and other city biographers. McKelvey published *Water-Power City* in "the heyday of the so-called 'consensus history.'" Shortly thereafter, the social sciences "began to have a marked influence upon the American historical profession." These practitioners would criticize the work of McKelvey and other city biographers for what Michael Frisch has described as their "idiosyncratic approach" to history.[40] Scholars such as Eric E. Lampard argued that urban historians should attempt to explain the process of urbanization within American society as a whole rather than focusing on individual cities. "American urban history—what there is of it—is largely the history of cities and their 'problems,' not the history of urbanization," Lampard wrote in 1961. "We do not know enough about urbanization or 'urban' characteristics in general to determine what is unique or otherwise in the experience of particular communities. The variant 'facts of history' cannot be defined nor their significance appraised until they are treated in relation to larger conceptual frameworks, yet the conventional type of local history, though monumental in detail, seldom furnishes data in forms that are readily adaptable to macroscopic treatment. We lack, therefore, not only generalized frameworks of analysis but consistent and comparable data relevant to them."[41]

Professionalizing Urban History

McKelvey didn't see a tension between the two points of view. For him, the in-depth study of individual cities was a necessary precursor to more comprehensive examinations of the processes of urbanization. "The task of urban historians," McKelvey argued in 1952, "is to chart the interrelated streams of life active in a specific community at a given period, or to weigh the cumulative effect in time of the problems and achievements of many cities within a given society, and in both cases to measure the extent to which the ideals and aspirations of that society found expression, growth, or rebirth in urban centers."[42] McKelvey did all of this. The second volume of his Rochester series was in production

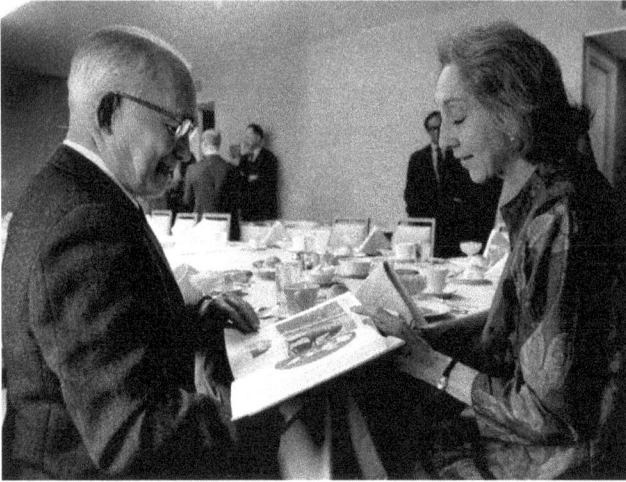

Blake McKelvey with Anita Leslie, grandniece of Lady Randolph Churchill, at a luncheon at the Flagship Hotel in Rochester, New York, in 1970. Photo by T. Gordon Massecar. *Courtesy of the Collection of the City Historian.*

when Perkins retired in 1948 and McKelvey was promoted to city historian. He produced two additional volumes after that, bringing his history of the city up through 1961. But he also built on the foundations he and other urban biographers had laid to engage in broader studies of urbanization and to support others who were doing so.[43] In 1963, just two years after completing his fourth and final volume of *Rochester*, McKelvey published *The Urbanization of America: 1860–1915*. It was among only a small group of publications available for use in urban history classrooms in the mid-1960s. Within ten years, he had completed three additional volumes on urbanization.[44]

This made him not only a pioneer in the field of urban history but also an influential leader. Michael H. Ebner described the early development of the field, and of McKelvey's role in it, in his 1981 retrospective. He noted that in 1952, only six scholars—Oscar Handlin, W. Stull Holt, Allan Nevins, Bessie Louise Pierce, Arthur M. Schlesinger Sr., and Bayrd Still—had taught or were teaching college-level courses about the history of American cities. But interest was growing. In 1953, recognizing the need for a forum for information sharing, McKelvey and Still convened a group of about fifteen scholars for the first meeting of the Urban History Group. Attendees "agreed to the desirability of exchanging information about research, sponsoring programs dealing with urban topics and issuing a newsletter," which, among other things, was useful for sharing syllabi for urban history courses.[45] The two-page mimeographed newsletter the group produced in its first year eventually transformed into the journal *Urbanism Past and Present*.[46] In addition to chairing the Urban History Group, McKelvey edited and published its newsletter from the city historian's office in the Rochester Public Library. He was chosen for the task because, among his peers in the field, he "was the only one at that time who had an office with a secretary."[47] The most recognized outlet for the study of urban history today, the *Journal of Urban History*, wasn't established until twenty years later, in 1974.

The "New Urban History"

During his long career in the city historian's office, McKelvey both witnessed and contributed not only to the emergence of the field of urban history but also to what some saw as its bifurcation into "traditional" and "new" social scientific approaches. Drawing on methods initiated in disciplines such as sociology and political science, scholars aligned with the "new urban history" relied on demographic and statistical analyses to identify the kinds of patterns in urban development that scholars like Lampart demanded. McKelvey didn't necessarily see a distinction. For him, it was a matter of selecting the proper tools and methods for one's purpose. Though McKelvey is generally classified as a "traditional" urban historian, he incorporated some social-scientific approaches into his studies, foreshadowing the potential for a "new urban history" that would greatly expand on such methodologies. He described himself as a "quantifier" who used quantitative research in *The Water-Power City* and his other studies, especially to understand changing demographics.[48] But he also recognized the limitations of his own work.

By the time McKelvey retired as the city historian in 1973, both the field of urban history and the role of the city historian had changed significantly. In welcoming his successor, Joseph W. Barnes, McKelvey acknowledged that new approaches to the study of history could provide insight that his own work had not. The "placid and depressed city" that had greeted him in the midst of the Great Depression in 1936 had "grown into a dynamic and prosperous metropolis."

> While it has lost its seeming tranquility and most of its noble elms, it has acquired in addition to new demographic and regional problems a new participatory vitality, which is abundantly evident in both civic and cultural institutional affairs. Historically it is therefore time for a shift from an emphasis on the city's expanding horizons to a quantitative examination of its internal structure and an interdisciplinary assessment of its character. This will require the direction of a younger scholar equipped with the skills requisite for the new approach.[49]

Born in 1945, the same year in which *The Water-Power City* was published, Barnes would see his scholarship influenced not only by urban history's pioneers like Schlesinger and McKelvey, but also by advocates of the "rigorous, empirical, and analytical approach" of "new urban historians."[50] When he was appointed the city historian, Barnes was completing a PhD at the University at Buffalo, where he was exposed to scholars who increasingly combined "conceptual approaches and rigorous quantification with the idiographic appeal of traditional history."[51] McKelvey had hired him into a temporary position as an assistant historian in 1972 to inventory and organize records in the city's archives and recommended him as his successor when he retired a year later. Barnes continued to play an important role in establishing the city's records management and archives program until an archivist was hired to oversee it.

Barnes served as the city historian for eleven years, but his work never attained the status that his predecessor's had, nor did it fully live up to the promise offered by new social-scientific approaches. He readily admitted that he was "not into the quantitative world of computers" that many of the new social and urban historians were embracing. Indeed, the body of written work that Barnes produced—fewer than two dozen *Rochester History* essays—while certainly adding to the body of knowledge about Rochester, differed little in type of subject matter, tone, or approach from McKelvey's. He tended to highlight businesses, civic organizations, and public-works projects, though he also occasionally looked at social change, such as the effects of immigration. Perhaps his most significant contribution was his series of articles, adapted from his doctoral dissertation, about the annexations that expanded Rochester's borders in the early twentieth century.[52] Barnes's focus and approach may have been due, in part, to McKelvey's shadow looming so large. Indeed, though McKelvey had retired, he remained a steady presence in the historian's office until his death in 2000. He continued to write books, as well as occasional articles for *Rochester History*, and cowrote (with Barnes) and narrated a film for local public television station WXXI, aptly titled *Blake McKelvey's Rochester*.[53]

Barnes's work was also affected by financial constraints and changing expectations for what it meant to be a city historian. As Barnes noted in an interview in 1984, the cost of publishing lengthy books such as Foreman's three volumes on World War I servicemen and McKelvey's four-volume history of Rochester had increased substantially. "It all comes down to money when you think in terms of official historical publications with a fairly narrow appeal," Barnes said. "The cost of hardcover books is out of sight. . . . These are different times, and they call for different approaches in telling the Rochester story."[54] Instead of writing lengthy textual pieces, Barnes found other ways of sharing history with the public. He collaborated with other cultural heritage institutions to produce exhibits, developed slide presentations—some delivered in person and some with accompanying audiotape recordings—and wrote mini biographies of prominent historical figures for a series of cards that were distributed during the city's sesquicentennial celebration in 1984. He also gave frequent presentations to senior-citizen groups and recorded oral history interviews with 200 longtime city residents.[55]

A More Public Turn

The "different approaches" that Barnes took—and which would become even more prevalent under his successors—represented yet another of the subfields within history that McKelvey is credited with helping to pioneer: public history. In the inaugural issue of *The Public Historian* in 1978, Robert Kelley offered this definition: "Public History refers to the employment of historians and the historical method outside of academia: in government, private corporations, the media, historical societies and museums, even in private practice."[56] McKelvey saw the imperative even more broadly—as history intended for a public audience or a public purpose. In his view, history could and should be not only accessible to but produced specifically for a public audience. Today, practitioners generally agree.[57] This is precisely what McKelvey did. From his first day on the job, he set out to produce history for "the Citizens of Rochester."[58]

When Barnes abruptly left his position as Rochester city historian in 1985, McKelvey hand-picked a replacement who shared his vision of building community through history. Ruth Rosenberg-Naparsteck first encountered Blake McKelvey while she was working on her master's degree in history as a student at the State University of New York (SUNY) Brockport. Unlike her mentor or her immediate predecessor, she never attained a PhD, but her enthusiasm caught McKelvey's attention. He took her on first as an intern, then as an assistant, before recommending her appointment as Barnes's replacement in 1987. Almost immediately, Rosenberg-Naparsteck's work had a different feel to it. It's difficult to say whether this was a deliberate choice or the result of circumstances that thrust her into a high-profile project right from the start. In July 1984, a bulldozer working in Highland Park unearthed half a dozen skeletons. Ultimately, archaeologists uncovered the remains of 305 people, all most likely residents of the city's poorhouse, insane asylum, and penitentiary.

Rosenberg-Naparsteck, then serving as the assistant city historian, immediately set out to learn as much as she could about the people who had seemingly been forgotten. She eventually was able to name 251 people who had died between 1847 and 1850 as inmates of one of the three facilities and who had almost certainly been buried at Highland Park. This research resulted in the first article that she authored for *Rochester History*, "Life and Death in Nineteenth Century Rochester."[59]

Rosenberg-Naparsteck would continue to highlight social movements and cultural issues throughout her career in the historian's office, embracing the "new social history" that sought to reconstruct history "from the bottom up" or from the perspective of "ordinary people," rather than the elite. She was particularly dedicated to expanding knowledge about women, immigrants, and people of color. The roughly twenty-five articles she wrote for the journal included examinations of the Kimball tobacco factory and the anti-tobacco movement and Rochester's response to the Vietnam War. As the editor of the journal, she published articles by others about

Former City Historian Ruth Rosenberg-Naparsteck examines a map in her office at the Rundel Memorial Building of the Central Library of Rochester & Monroe County, 1996. *From the collection of the Rochester Public Library Local History & Genealogy Division.*

abolitionist Frederick Douglass, baseball, Civil War soldiers, World War II plant workers, immigrants, and Rochester's ethnic neighborhoods. But it wasn't just the subject matter that made Rosenberg-Naparsteck's approach different. The audience had changed, and the style and tone of the historian's work followed suit. When McKelvey began his career in Rochester, print was still the dominant means of communicating information, most photography was still black and white, and the city's only radio stations were AM. The city's first television station didn't go on air until 1949, and then only in black and white.[60]

By the mid-1980s, when Rosenberg-Naparsteck began her tenure as historian, Rochesterians—like most Americans—had access to a much wider and more vivid array of media than ever before. In addition to two daily newspapers, Rochester had numerous AM and FM radio stations and several over-the-air television stations, all broadcasting in color. Those who could afford to subscribe to cable television had even more choices. Text-dense tomes like McKelvey's *Rochester* series no longer appealed to the broad public audience for which it had been intended. "We're always looking for new ways to get to people," Rosenberg-Naparsteck said. "A lot of people think they don't like history and they don't want to pick up a history book."[61] Understanding this, in 1979 McKelvey embraced Rochester's reputation as the "Image City" and produced a glossy, full-color coffee-table-style picture book, *A Panoramic History of Rochester and Monroe County, New York*, showing, rather than telling, readers what the city looked like in the past.[62] Rosenberg-Naparsteck continued this trend, publishing three picture books of her own: *Rochester: A Pictorial History* (1989), *Runnin' Crazy: A Portrait of the Genesee* River (1996) (coauthored with Edward P. Curtis Jr.), and *Historic Photos of Rochester* (2007), as well as an updated version of McKelvey's *A Panoramic History* (2001).

Those would be the last books produced by the city's historian. By the early 2000s, Americans were getting more and more of their information from online sources. The return on investment in longform print publications—measured as much by reach and increase in community knowledge as by profit—was no longer guaranteed. At the same time, a series of economic recessions prompted the City to look for efficiencies and cost-cutting measures. The historian's role was combined with that of the archivist and records manager in 2004, and Rosenberg-Naparsteck was tasked with day-to-day oversight of the City of Rochester's entire records management program. Then, in June 2007, the city council voted to eliminate the position of full-time historian altogether, and Rosenberg-Naparsteck was let go. The city was deliberately without a historian for the first time in eighty-six years. The city council took a year to "study possibilities for reorganizing, outsourcing, or partnering with someone in the community to keep the historian at a much reduced salary" so that it could meet its obligations under the state's Historian's Law.[63] A year later, they decided that the job could be done by a part-time library assistant at a salary of approximately $20,000 per year. I was appointed to the position in October 2008.[64]

With the city celebrating its 175th anniversary in 2009, my first assignment was to develop content for an interactive web-based timeline of Rochester's history and assist with other aspects of the commemoration. Within a year, the historian's office resumed responsibility for publishing *Rochester History*, which had temporarily been managed by the Rochester Historical Society in the absence of an appointed historian, and I took over as its editor. In 2012, the part-time position of historian was combined with the full-time job of managing the library's local history and digitization departments. I have been employed full-time since then.

Still, my job as city historian is very different from McKelvey's. While I continue to edit (and very occasionally write for) *Rochester History*, most of my time is spent engaging directly with the public, answering questions in person and through email and phone calls, and giving public presentations and media interviews. Instead of writing books, I produce short-form content for walking tours, interpretive signs, exhibits, websites, blogs, and, increasingly, social media. I am frequently consulted by local, national, and, occasionally, international news reporters and media producers and have appeared in numerous documentary films, most produced by local public broadcasting affiliate WXXI. I even appeared in a 2012 episode of the SyFy Channel's *Ghost Hunters*.[65]

Despite the differences, my aim remains the same as McKelvey's—to build community by connecting residents through an understanding of the past. Like Rosenberg-Naparsteck, I have sought to uplift the stories of traditionally marginalized people, including women, people of color, and those who identify as LGBTQ+. In 2017, I co-curated a major exhibit commemorating the 100th anniversary of New York

Christine L. Ridarsky, Rochester and Monroe County Historian. *From the City of Rochester.*

State recognizing women's right to vote. In 2019, I served as the director and lead curator of an internationally lauded community-curated exhibit marking the fiftieth anniversary of the uprising at the Stonewall Inn that launched the modern LGBTQ+ rights movement. In 2021, I helped launch an Archive of Black History & Culture at the library. I have also directed several projects designed to record interviews with residents, including the Rochester-Monroe County Vietnam-Era Veterans Oral History Project, which captured the stories of more than seventy area veterans.

In December 2024, my job changed again when I was appointed to the additional position of Monroe County Historian. It is the first time a single full-time person has served both the city and the county. This presents exciting

opportunities to connect urban, suburban, and rural residents by encouraging them to explore both shared and divergent pasts. This year, Rochester, Monroe County, and New York State are commemorating the bicentennial of the Erie Canal's opening in 1825. Next year marks the 250th anniversary of the Declaration of Independence and the Revolutionary War. We will mark several more local anniversaries in coming years, including the centennials of the county park system and the county's airport, culminating in the City of Rochester's bicentennial in 2034. Nearly ninety years after Blake McKelvey first set foot in Rochester, there is still much to learn about the community's history. Fortunately, he left a legacy upon which we can continue to build.

Conclusion

Toward the end of his career, McKelvey recalled what he described as the best compliment he had ever received. It came not from another scholar but from a plumber who was working in his house. "Are you *the* Blake McKelvey?'" the workman asked. "'I'm the only one I know of,'" McKelvey answered. "'Well then I've been reading your books for about fifteen years,'" the plumber told him.[66] McKelvey had achieved his greatest goal. From the very beginning, McKelvey set out to write history that had meaning for the citizens of Rochester. For him, history was a tool to be used to build community in the present. As the narrator in the 1976 film *Blake McKelvey's Rochester* put it, "One purpose of his effort has been to show that what came before explains where we are today, and that what we do today will determine the shape of tomorrow."[67] Eighty years after he published *The Water-Power City* and nearly a quarter century after his death, Blake McKelvey continues to provide a service to the citizens of Rochester. The massive body of work he produced during his lifetime—at least two dozen books and more than a hundred articles for the *Rochester History* journal, not to mention the many essays he published elsewhere—remains the foremost source of information on Rochester's history. McKelvey's legacy can also be found in the deep and abiding pride that citizens take in Rochester's history. As Mark Hare wrote in 2007, the work of Rochester's historians "creates a sense of place and who we are that many communities lack."[68]

Acknowledgments

I would like to thank Bruce Leslie for his insightful questions and helpful feedback on early drafts of this essay and for his enduring friendship, mentorship, and support. ■

1. Blake F. McKelvey, *Rochester: The Water-Power City, 1812–1854* (Harvard University Press, 1945).
2. For example, see Aaron I. Abell in *Revista de Historia de América*, no. 22 (December 1946): 492, https://www.jstor.org/stable/20137561; David Maldwyn Ellis, *The Mississippi Valley Historical Review* 32, no. 4 (March 1946): 607–8. https://www.jstor.org/stable/1895261; and William Miller, *The Journal of Economic History* 7, no. 1 (May 1947): 95–96, https://www.jstor.org/stable/2113610.
3. McKelvey, *Water-Power City*, v.
4. For the original text of the law, see New York State, *Laws of 1919*. The law has been amended several times since 1919 and is currently embodied in Arts and Cultural Affairs, article 57, § 13, 15, 17. The Historian's Law excluded counties from the mandate, but the position is required under County Law, § 400 4 (a). For discussion on the law and the state's municipal and county historians, see Carol Kammen, "On Doing Local History in New York State: New York's Municipal Historians," *New York History* 69, no. 1 (January 1988): 99–113, https://www.jstor.org/stable/23178489; and Kammen, "On the Doing of Local History in New York," *The Public Historian* 33, no. 3 (Summer 2011): 58–69, https://www.jstor.org/stable/10.1525/tph.2011.33.3.58.
5. "Edward R. Foreman Dies, Noted as City's Historian," *Democrat & Chronicle*, February 23, 1936.
6. Edward R. Foreman, ed., *World War Service Record of Rochester and Monroe County, New York*, 3 vols. (The DuBois Press, 1924–1930).
7. Review, *The Quarterly Journal of the New York State Historical Association* 12, no. 1 (January 1931): 74, https://www.jstor.org/stable/43566214.
8. Henry O'Reilly, *Settlement in the West: Sketches of Rochester: With Incidental Notices of Western New-York* (William Alling, 1838); Dexter Perkins, "Henry O'Reilly," *Rochester History* 7, no. 1 (January 1945): 6. For a more critical review of *Sketches*, see McKelvey, "A History of Historical Writing in the Rochester Area," *Rochester History* 6, no. 2 (April 1944): 3–5.
9. Dexter Perkins, *Yield of the Years: An Autobiography* (Little, Brown, and Co., 1969), 75; "London, Rochester Honor Dr. Perkins," *Democrat & Chronicle*, June 3, 1936. The salary comparison is based on the US Bureau of Labor Statistics Consumer Product Index (CPI) Inflation Calculator, accessed March 1, 2025, https://www.bls.gov/data/inflation_calculator.htm.
10. J. Sheldon Fisher, "Tip of the hat to historians who hold open door to the past," *Democrat & Chronicle*, September 26, 2000.
11. "Historian Blake F. McKelvey dies at 97," *Democrat & Chronicle*, September 14, 2000.
12. Bruce M. Stave, "A Conversation with Blake McKelvey," in *The Making of the Urban History: Historiography Through Oral History* (Sage, 1977), 33–62.
13. Stave, 36–37.
14. Stave, 34–36.
15. Arthur M. Schlesinger, *In Retrospect: The History of a Historian* (Harcourt, Brace & World, 1963), 68, 113.
16. Andrea Tuttle Kornbluh. Review of Schlesinger, Arthur Meier, *The Rise of the City, 1878–1898* (H-Urban, H-Net Reviews. September 1998), http://www.h-net.org/reviews/showrev.php?id=2344; Arthur M. Schlesinger, "The City in American History," *Mississippi Valley Historical Review*, no. XXVII (June 1940), 43–66.
17. Stave, 17–18.
18. McKelvey, *American Prisons: A Study in American Social History Prior to 1915* (University of Chicago Press, 1933).
19. McKelvey, *Water-Power City*, xi.
20. Schlesinger, *"The Rise of the City*, 448, as quoted in McKelvey, "American Urban History Today," *The American Historical Review* 57, no. 4 (July 1952): 919.

21. In addition to *Water-Power City*, these included *The Flower City, 1855–1890* (1949), *The Quest for Quality, 1890–1925* (1956), and *An Emerging Metropolis, 1925–1961* (1961).

22. Bruce M. Stave, *The Making of Urban History: Historiography Through Oral History* (Sage, 1977), 38–39.

23. McKelvey, "A City Historian's Report," *Rochester History* 35, no. 3 (July 1973): 7.

24. McKelvey, "City Historian's Report," 1–2.

25. "Historian Aide Will Prepare City Volume," *Democrat & Chronicle*, July 7, 1936. The salary comparison is based on the US Bureau of Labor Statistics Consumer Product Index (CPI) Inflation Calculator, https://www.bls.gov/data/inflation_calculator.htm.

26. The Office of the City Historian and the Rochester Public Library continued to publish four issues per year through 2006, each generally consisting of a single essay. Publication became more sporadic beginning in 2007 when the job of city historian was temporarily eliminated and then reestablished as a part-time position. The journal was reinvigorated in 2023 through a partnership between the Office of the City Historian, the Rochester Public Library, Rochester Institute of Technology's History Department, and RIT Press—resulting in the current format. The journal is now published twice yearly, spring and fall, by RIT Press. In addition to the well-researched essays for which it has come to be known, the new format includes a variety of additional print and digital content, including book and exhibit reviews, feature articles that highlight unique artifacts, and discussions about teaching in K–12 and college classrooms. https://rochesterhistory.rit.edu/.

27. McKelvey, "City Historian's Report," 4.

28. The journal continues to be subsidized by the Frances Kenyon Publication Fund, established in memory of Ms. Kenyon's sister Florence Taber Kenyon and her friend Thelma Jeffries.

29. See *Rochester History*, Table of Contents, accessed March 1, 2025, https://roccitylibrary.org/digital-collections/rochester-history/rochester-history-table-of-contents/.

30. McKelvey, "City Historian's Report," 9.

31. Stave, 43–44.

32. Stave, 44. The volumes to which McKelvey referred were Bessie Louise Pierce, *A History of Chicago, Volume 1: The Beginning of a City, 1673–1848* (A. A. Knopf, 1937); *Volume 2: From Town to City, 1848–1871* (A. A. Knopf, 1940); *Volume 3: The Rise of a Modern City, 1871–1893* (A. A. Knopf, 1957); Constance Green, *Holyoke, Massachusetts: A Case History of the Industrial Revolution in America* (Yale University Press, 1939); Gerald M. Capers Jr., *The Biography of a River Town: Memphis: Its Heroic Age* (University of North Carolina Press, 1939).

33. Stave, 18.

34. Dorothy Culp, Review of *Rochester: The Water-Power City, 1812–1854*, *The American Historical Review* 51, no. 3 (April 1946): 515–16, https://www.jstor.org/stable/1840132.

35. Glyndon G. Van Deusen, Review of *Rochester: The Water-Power City, 1812–1854*, *New York History* 27, no. 2 (April 1946): 244–46, https://www.jstor.org/stable/23149601.

36. Letter, Joe L. Norris to Blake McKelvey, March 19, 1947. Office of the City Historian Records, Series III, Box 44.

37. Stave, 45.

38. McKelvey, "American Urban History Today," *The American Historical Review* 57, no. 4 (July 1952): 919.

39. The Minnesota Historical Society Press produced a series of urban biographies in the early 2020s that included Duluth, Minneapolis, and Rochester. See, for example, Virginia M. Wright-Peterson, *Rochester: An Urban Biography* (Minnesota Historical Society Press, 2022).

40. Michael Frisch, "American Urban History as an Example of Recent Historiography," *History and Theory* 18, no. 3 (October 1979): 352–54.

41. Eric E. Lampard, "American Historians and the Study of Urbanization," *The American Historical Review* 67, no. 1 (October 1961): 54, https://www.jstor.org/stable/1846261.

42. McKelvey, "American Urban History Today," 920.

43. The second volume was already in production at the time of McKelvey's appointment, which was effective May 1, 1948. For news of McKelvey's ascension, see "McKelvey to Be Historian for City; Succeeds Perkins," April 2, 1948.

44. McKelvey, *The Urbanization of America: 1860-1915* (Rutgers University Press, 1963); *The Emergence of Metropolitan America, 1915-1966* (Rutgers University Press, 1968); *The City in American History* (George Allen & Unwin, 1969); *American Urbanization: A Comparative History* (Scott, Foresman and Co., 1973).

45. Bruce M. Stave, "Introduction," in *The Making of the Urban History: Historiography Through Oral History* (Sage, 1977), 14-15.

46. Stave, 14, 16.

47. Stave, 48. The history of The Urban History Group newsletter is recounted in Blake McKelvey and A. Theodore Brown, "The Urban History Group Newsletter," *Urbanism Past & Present* 1 (Winter 1975-1976): 36-37, https://www.jstor.org/stable/44403505.

48. Stave, 20.

49. McKelvey, "City Historian's Report," 24.

50. Michael Frisch, "American Urban History as an Example of Recent Historiography," *History and Theory* 18, no. 3 (October 1979): 352-54.

51. Frisch, 356.

52. See Joseph W. Barnes, "The Annexation of Brighton Village," *Rochester History* 35, no. 1 (January 1973); and "The Annexation of Charlotte," *Rochester History* 37, no. 1 (January 1975).

53. This film can be viewed in the digital version of the journal.

54. "His Place Is in History," *Democrat & Chronicle*, April 22, 1984.

55. "City Historian: I'd Like This Job for Life," *Democrat & Chronicle*, March 19, 1976; "His Place is in History," *Democrat & Chronicle*, April 22, 1984. The oral history interviews that Barnes recorded are preserved as part of the historian's archives. They were recorded on cassette tapes and have not yet been digitized, so access is somewhat limited.

56. Robert Kelley, "Public History: Its Origins, Nature, and Prospects," *The Public Historian* 1, no. 1 (Autumn 1978), https://www.jstor.org/stable/3377666. McKelvey is acknowledged as a pioneer in the field in the "Editor's Preface," 9: "For we are not saying that only now are Public Historians being trained in the new graduate programs; for the past several decades, historians such as Hewlett, Rasmussen, Blake McKelvey (city historian of Rochester), Lawrence Bruser (Mitsui Corporation historian) and others have led the way. They need to be recognized and their experience needs to be brought to the attention of the aspirants to this new field."

57. Charles C. Cole Jr., "Public History: What Difference Has It Made?" *The Public Historian* 16, no. 4 (Autumn 1994): 9-35.

58. In 1984, during Rochester's sesquicentennial, McKelvey also published a much-condensed version of his four-volume series. Dedicated "to the Citizens of Rochester," it summarized the city's history in a mere ninety-four pages, including a chapter entitled "A Grass-Roots Metropolis: 1965-1984" that covered the period after his original series concluded. McKelvey, *Rochester: A Brief History* (The Edwin Mellen Press, 1984). He also discussed his goal of reaching a public, as opposed to a purely academic, audience in his interview with Staves, noted elsewhere in this article.

59. Ruth Rosenberg-Naparsteck, "Life and Death in Nineteenth Century Rochester," *Rochester History* 45, nos. 1 and 2 (July and October 1983) (though dated in 1983, this issue of the journal was not actually published until 1985).

60. See Blake McKelvey, "Radio and Television in the Life of Rochester," *Rochester History* 32, no. 3.

61. Elizabeth Forbes, "Devour history over lunch at Brown's Race lecture series," *Democrat & Chronicle*, January 8, 1994.

62. McKelvey, *Rochester: A Panoramic History of Rochester and Monroe County, New York* (Windsor, 1979).

63. Mark Hare, "Cutting city historian to save money is backward," *Democrat & Chronicle*, June 28, 2007.

64. In 2012, the role of part-time city historian was combined with the position of manager of the Rochester Public Library's Local History & Genealogy Division, creating one full-time job. I held that position until December 2024, when the previously separate part-time positions of Rochester and Monroe County historians were combined into a single full-time job and split from the library role. I am now employed full-time, serving half-time as city historian and half-time as county historian.

65. *Ghost Hunters*, season 8, episode 25, "Due Date with Death," SyFy Channel. Aired November 28, 2012.

66. Stave, 58.

67. Blake F. McKelvey and Joseph W. Barnes, "'Blake McKelvey's Rochester': Script from a One-Hour Film Documentary," *Rochester History* 38, no. 1 (January 1976): 5.

68. Hare, *Democrat & Chronicle*, June 28, 2007.

The Completists
Blake McKelvey, Bessie Louise Pierce,
and Urban Biography

Michael Brown

G rowing up the son of a Methodist minister, Blake McKelvey moved among several locations in the mountainous middle of Pennsylvania that arcs from Philadelphia to Pittsburgh. Looking back on his early days decades later, he particularly remembered two of these places: Huntingdon and, later, at the time of high school, Williamsport. The former sits astride the Juniata River and the latter along the West Branch of the Susquehanna. Both are in valleys, with ground rising fast around them. Such topography offered McKelvey, literally, his first perspective on cities.[1]

McKelvey recalled how in Huntingdon his father "would take us Sunday afternoons on a hike to a hill from which we could see the city. Of course, he was always pointing out the number of churches, and I remember looking down, identifying the churches and seeing the court house, the jail, the railroad station, and the high school." In Williamsport, McKelvey sought such vistas himself. "I can remember when we first arrived that I got a bicycle and rode out to the edge of town to see the amusement center there, and then to the resort area at the other end. I rode across the bridge to where you could climb a hill and see the whole town. I remember this curiosity about cities." In these formative moments, when his interest in them was first kindled, cities were a thing McKelvey could see entirely, in one view.[2]

A Distinctive Career Path
In his professional work on the history of Rochester, which began when he arrived in 1936 to take the position of assistant city historian and which concluded not so much with his retirement in 1973 as his death in 2000, McKelvey

Michael Brown is an associate professor of history and a faculty affiliate in the Museum Studies Program at Rochester Institute of Technology.

A circa 1913 panoramic view of Huntingdon, Pennsylvania, where McKelvey spent part of his childhood. *From Library of Congress Prints and Photographs Division.*

would, over the course of sixty-four years of research and writing, develop another sort of vantage point from which to see a city seemingly in its entirety. His long tenure in Rochester and at the city historian's office, McKelvey wrote in 1989, "enabled me to produce the only complete historical biography of a city yet written in America or abroad."[3] McKelvey's full survey of Rochester, a four-volume "urban biography," became his best-known work.[4]

By all accounts a humble man, McKelvey was not crowning himself with laurels but rather pointing to the singularity of his career. As the urban historian Bayrd Still noted in 1977, four years after McKelvey's retirement:

> Individual authorship of a comprehensive history or "biography" of any major city has now become an unrealistic pursuit for at least two reasons. Most cities are too large, and scholars (economists, social historians, geographers, and political scientists) are asking too many questions. The city biographers attempted to comprehend the whole span of a city's history, but in the case of most cities this has become an insuperable task, especially if one cannot give undivided attention, for a long period of time, to the project. Blake McKelvey was able to do this for Rochester, a city that had a shorter life span than some (roughly since 1812) and that is less sizable than many. As City Historian of Rochester, McKelvey worked almost uninterruptedly on the project for at least fifteen years.[5]

The "project" was McKelvey's four-volume *Rochester*, published between 1945 and 1961. Still could point to only one other work that, in seeking to produce a

complete city history, rivaled McKelvey's: University of Chicago historian Bessie Louise Pierce's three-volume history of Chicago (a projected fourth was never finished), published across twenty years, 1937 to 1957. "Bessie Pierce told me," Still recalled, "that in the preparation of the first two volumes of her history of Chicago she had the assistance annually of from two to ten graduate students working from a third to full time over a period of about ten years."[6] One of those assistants, with a newly minted PhD from Harvard and a pressing need for a paycheck, was Blake McKelvey.[7]

****

Blake McKelvey's long career may be understood in the context of the legacy of the Progressive historians and the wider Progressive movement, the development of urban history as a field, the professionalization of local history, and the annals of what we now call public history.[8] Uniting these several elements was McKelvey's belief in the civic value of history and the desire to do civically significant historical research. McKelvey extolled and exemplified the proposition that historical work had public value, and his career highlights an institutional setting in which to produce such work: the office of municipal historian. While these aspects of McKelvey's story may be fairly well known (due in part to McKelvey's published reflections about them), less examined are the formal means of realizing his vision: What sort of output best fitted both his civic aspirations and his institutional location?

For McKelvey, the answer was urban "biography," represented by the four-volume *Rochester*, which stands, arguably, at the center of his life's work.

McKelvey's vision for urban biography owed an intellectual and a professional debt to Pierce and her ambitious History of Chicago Project. Initially a means of marking the city's centennial, the Chicago Project "as recast by Pierce . . . became a complex effort to survey all relevant historical records for a definitive four-volume account of Chicago's growth from 1673 to 1915."[9] It was the blueprint for McKelvey's work on Rochester, which he would later characterize as "the only complete" such work in existence.[10] The version of history best suited to civic purposes, McKelvey and Pierce indicated by their work, was a completist one.

McKelvey's vision of complete urban histories is ripe for critical reassessment. Is the complete history of a city possible, and if so, what constitutes it? Is the completist's aim itself a problem, given the pervasiveness of academic and public histories that excluded (and) marginalized people, but nonetheless claimed the mantle of being complete? If complete urban biography is neither possible nor desirable, then how much city history—how much of the steady accumulation of facts, such as those about Rochester that McKelvey published over a lifetime—is required to reach the threshold of civic value?

Comprehensive urban histories, particularly the "city biography" approach that McKelvey used, have been subject to vigorous debate among scholars. On the one hand, McKelvey was part of a generation of urban historians whose city biographies were hailed as a scholarly advance relative to the writing about cities that preceded them. "Antiquarians, ancestor worshippers, and addicts of 'colorful' history will be disappointed in this volume," a 1950 reviewer of McKelvey's second book, *Rochester: The Flower City, 1855–1890*, declared. "Serious students of the great period of urban development in America will find it a rewarding study solidly based on the newspapers, the chamber of commerce reports, the city's printed records, and upon those admirable studies which the local historical society has promoted in recent years. Let us hope that other cities will find historians to tell their stories on a similar scale and with like skill."[11]

By the 1960s, however, a new generation of historians looked upon urban biographies as retrograde—lacking analytical heft. "So long as urban history remains a rubric under which can be placed all things that happened in cities, progress [in the academic field] is more than likely to be impeded," observed Theodore Hershberg, a professor of history and public policy at the University of Pennsylvania, in 1978. "To move ahead it will be necessary to grasp the fundamental distinction between the treatment of urban as site and urban as process, to differentiate the study of the city as a dependent and an independent variable, to systematically explore the relationships between behavior and environment, and to understand the consequences arising from the failure to distinguish between urban and social history." Hershberg found that city histories such as Pierce's and McKelvey's, "though carefully researched and well-written, lack any significant conceptual framework or fail in their periodization schema to distinguish adequately between urban and national history."[12]

Historian for the Public

While McKelvey was trained as a scholar (though not in urban history, specifically) and participated quite actively in scholarly life, he understood that his work on Rochester was not only for—nor, indeed, primarily for—other scholars. "My first obligation is to the citizens of Rochester whose interest in the community's history has fostered this study," he wrote in the acknowledgments for his first volume, *Rochester: The Water-Power City, 1812–1854*, published in 1945 by Harvard University Press. That obligation was material, for as then–City Historian Dexter Perkins noted in the preface, given McKelvey's municipal position, the book "represents if not a unique, at any rate a most striking, achievement, the preparation of a history of an important American city on the basis of careful research, exact scholarship, and expert judgment all provided for by municipal funds." Financial support for McKelvey's work included the Rochester Public Library's Kate Gleason Fund—established by and named for a leading figure in Rochester and, ultimately, global business, banking, engineering, manufacturing, building, and philanthropic endeavors. Upon her death in 1933, Gleason "endowed the History Division of the Rochester Public Library as a memorial for Amelia Brettelle, her teacher of history in the public schools. To expand the usefulness of the bequest even beyond gathering historical records, and to encourage a forward look through the past," the trust included money for publications. Supported by these funds and employed by the city, McKelvey produced what Perkins called "a remarkable municipal achievement."[13]

A circa 1941 portrait of City Historian Dexter Perkins by J. Ernest Mock. *Courtesy of University Archives Photograph Collection, UA915, Rare Books, Special Collections, and Preservation, River Campus Libraries, University of Rochester.*

McKelvey's obligation to Rochester was moral as well as material: He intended his history to have some public benefit. He understood that writing for a broader public might mean that his work would not keep pace with academics operating at the edges of the field of urban history. "It should be noted that my studies of Rochester particularly have been written not for scholars, but for the city," he told an interviewer. "I've written them to be read by citizens in Rochester, and I have not been trying to prove a thesis; I've not been trying to demonstrate new insights into any subject. I've been trying to recreate the experiences of that community, growing into a modern city."[14]

For McKelvey, historical awareness of the kind he hoped to offer Rochesterians fit into a broader pattern of civic life. He highlighted the role of individuals in shaping history, often in a way that valorized their efforts. At times, McKelvey presented this view as an article of faith—a hope about the way the world could and should work. At other times, he offered it as an empirical observation—a historian's take on how the world did, in fact, function. Sometimes, he blended these elements. The year after completing his biography of Rochester, McKelvey wrote that in historical development

> each movement forward or backward was, in my judgment, the work of individual citizens whether many or few. Their ability to plan and act together is a widely shared human quality manifested in formal and informal aspects of the democratic society of which we are a part and which we can help to reshape, if not exactly in accordance with our ideals, at least in our own image. The activity of such a dynamic society is the substance of history, and its continued existence is the historian's faith.[15]

In a world where historical outcomes were shaped by individual thinking, choosing, and doing, historians' "search for underlying and motivating themes serves, when successful, to identify cooperative purposes and social goals that will liberate readers from a frustrating sense of chaos or the needless repetition of outmoded custom," McKelvey wrote. History could enliven citizens' sense of their own creative powers, and McKelvey "hope[d] that my volumes on Rochester will partially serve this purpose."[16]

In 1993, toward the end of his life and as he released the second edition of *Rochester on the Genesee: The Growth of a City*—a one-volume summary of his four-volume set—McKelvey pointed to two distinctive historical features of Rochester into which his own work might fit. One was "its spirit of self-criticism." The other was a belief, dating back to the powerful religious movements coursing through the city in the middle nineteenth century, "that man's fate is not preordained and that salvation is attainable by all who devoutly seek." This idea had over time "acquired a more secular interpretation—that we are free and responsible citizens." With a complete history of their city offered in that self-critical tradition, Rochesterians would be equipped to set the course of their community in the years ahead. "Thus the future of Rochester will be determined," McKelvey declared, offering a moral mission as much as an empirical prediction, "by its inhabitants."[17] His life's work was to aid that civic enterprise, and it raises the question: What kinds of city histories best meet the needs of "free and responsible citizens," and where does the completist approach initiated by Pierce and exemplified by McKelvey fit?

****

Pierce and a History of Chicago

Already recognized as a scholar on pedagogy and, perhaps, its antithesis—ideological propaganda—Bessie Louise Pierce arrived at the University of Chicago in 1929 under the auspices of the multidisciplinary Local Community Research Committee. She had earned her PhD in history in 1923, working with Arthur M. Schlesinger Sr. when he was at the University of Iowa. A decade later, Schlesinger would be McKelvey's advisor at Harvard. At Chicago, Pierce became an associate professor of history and the director of the History of Chicago Project, originally intended to mark the city's centennial (1933 or 1937, depending on the particular incorporation date held up as a point of origin). The project "was intended to integrate economic, political, and sociological studies already sponsored by the Committee and uncover new areas for further research."[18] In Pierce's hands, it became something more ambitious: a comprehensive history of Chicago.

Pierce's project was one of McKelvey's inspirations; his time working with her shaped his methods. Assigned to "research on the period of Chicago during the [1893] World's Fair," McKelvey "looked through the newspapers for two and a half years" and drafted 100 pages of material that Pierce reworked "until it was unrecognizable in the third volume." McKelvey sympathized with the challenges facing Pierce, who "had that enormous city to study, that large staff to direct but worst of all she had a big committee looking over her shoulder; every draft she finished had to go the rounds and satisfy all of the various interdisciplinary approaches." Later, when McKelvey "determined to write a new, independent, one-man history of Rochester," the scope of Pierce's project, if not the number of

A circa 1907 image of the University of Chicago, where McKelvey worked as a researcher for the Chicago Project under Bessie Louise Pierce. *From Library of Congress Prints and Photographs Division.*

its personnel, was on his mind. "I wanted to make a complete study," McKelvey recalled. "I had read Bessie Pierce's volumes. I don't know to what extent that influenced me, but I also remember eagerly looking at the early histories of other towns as they came out."[19] His connections to Pierce's Chicago Project highlight just how distinctive McKelvey was: He participated in both of the landmark, comprehensive city-history projects in the mid-twentieth century United States, with only his Rochester "biography" reaching the aim, as he put it, of being "complete."

When Pierce died in 1974, the project she had begun in 1929 remained incomplete. The third volume of her Chicago history was published in 1957, but the fourth would remain unfinished, slowed by "reductions in the size of the staff, Pierce's advancing age, and her practice of commuting regularly between Chicago and Iowa City in order to spend as much time as possible with her sister."[20] Even as her third volume neared publication, Pierce had already recognized the flaws of her completist approach. In a 1954 letter to Elsie M. Lewis, Pierce warned the younger historian not to follow her method. Lewis had earned her PhD in history at Chicago in 1946 and would go on to chair the history department at Howard University and to become the first Black woman to publish in the *Journal of Southern History*.[21] "My mistake has been, and still is," Pierce told Lewis, "that there is some impelling force which moves me to finish all that I can get my hands on in research before analyzing what I have and trying to write. With a mass of materials available on any worthwhile subject, I am sure that no one can hope to complete all that is available. The most any of us can do is to analyze after having sifted and then, when writing, plug any gaps which one may find." Pierce planned in her final volume "to do this very thing, but I am pretty old to change my ways. You are still young and can do so." Pierce's warning was "not a plea for superficiality . . . but it is a suggestion . . . that you can very well not exhaust everything and still do a first-class job."[22] Advising a move away from a completist's approach, Pierce also provided a definition of it: "Exhaust everything."

By "everything," Pierce had in mind sources—the "mass of materials" on Chicago. McKelvey, similarly, conceived of his plan to write a complete biography of Rochester as he became acquainted with the wealth of sources at his disposal in the city historian's office, which "adjoined" the Local History Division in the Rochester Public Library's Rundel Memorial Building. "In the course of compiling and editing . . . annual volumes for the Rochester Historical Society as well as the quarterly issues of [the journal] *Rochester History*, I had made a probing examination of the historical books and manuscripts assembled over several decades by the Society and now on deposit, together with the Library's own collections," McKelvey recalled. "My work with the National Youth Administration newspaper indexing project had prompted me to undertake, with the aid of my research assistants, a systematic reading of the back volumes of all Rochester papers. And since the unbroken files of these publications served as an invaluable community diary, I was able to produce what some urban historians elsewhere have characterized as a city biography."[23] McKelvey read one newspaper "for every day in every year." He "switched from one to another every six months or so because for many decades we had six newspapers, and I wanted to get the point of view of each one."[24]

Complete versus Whole

In the face of abundant historical sources for a city, the completists' task became the Herculean one of processing it all. As Bayrd Still put it, Bessie Pierce "was attempting to treat each aspect of the city's history as one would do in a doctoral dissertation, and then boil it all down to a comprehensible or manageable narrative, even in terms of four volumes. And the city was just too big and too complex to make that possible, even though she had many skilled professional people helping her. . . . Blake McKelvey had an easier job in that Rochester is smaller; since he could give virtually his whole attention to this, he was able within a lifetime to do the job." This undertaking was gargantuan, Still claimed, even before the advent of more social scientific approaches to urban history—the so-called new urban history of the middle 1960s and after—placed additional demands on sources and those sifting them. "The fact that new questions are now being asked," Still concluded, "make[s] the work of providing a comprehensive biography of a city more difficult because they open additional areas of inquiry."[25]

McKelvey was lauded for how fully he seemed to have processed all the sources related to Rochester. "McKelvey has earned a reputation as a human archive of local history," profiler Deborah Fineblum Raub wrote in the *Democrat & Chronicle* in 1999.[26] A 1974 review of his one-volume, consolidated history of Rochester characterized it as reflecting "his encyclopedic knowledge of the city." This same reviewer, University of Connecticut historian Estelle F. Feinstein, noted, however, that a complete survey of available sources is by no means a complete history of a city. "The wealth of detail (and a hasty glance at the earlier multivolume history) indicate a heavy reliance on newspapers, commercial directories, and records of chambers of commerce, city councils, churches, and similar municipal establishments." The result was "an old-fashioned, narrative, urban biography that takes the value of growth and the dominant role of parochial notables for granted. Entrepreneurial successes, large and small, and cultural happenings are assiduously recorded for each twenty-year period." Feinstein found McKelvey's work encyclopedic, in other words, but incomplete. "More critical, more rigorous, more conceptually-oriented historians," she wrote, "will have to examine, for themselves, such 'problems and responses' as the experiences of minorities in Rochester, the delivery of municipal services, the patterns of mobility, and the resolution of conflicts."[27]

Ironically, Pierce and McKelvey, in aiming for complete city histories, had been trying to overcome the very kinds of blinkered history that Feinstein charged McKelvey with having produced. Though the term "new social history" is most often associated with historiography in the 1960s and after, historians writing in earlier decades, like McKelvey and Pierce, were also quite consciously attempting to create a new history from the bottom up. Constance McLaughlin Green, an urban historian of McKelvey's generation and, like him, one whose books addressed single cities, wrote an influential 1940 essay on local history as a means of breaking important new ground. "American history in the past has been written from the top down, an approach feasible enough as long as scholars were content to write only political and diplomatic history," she noted. "But the necessity of studying American life from the bottom up becomes obvious for the cultural historian"—the latter her term for social history. "The story of how American people have lived as individuals and as communities must be told by details." Such work was "local history simon pure"; it was "the life history of a community."[28]

Pierce and McKelvey set out to write such history, with their shared teacher, Schlesinger, as an influence. Schlesinger considered "the shift from 'drum and trumpet history' to 'the history of culture, the real history of men and women'" to be "the most significant development in American historical study."[29] The in-depth study of individual cities offered Pierce and McKelvey a prime opportunity to write this more complete version of the American past, and both of them pointed to Schlesinger's "helpful" and "constructive" criticism of their manuscripts.[30] "Without ignoring the leaders of politics, finance, business, and intellectual endeavor," Pierce wrote in the preface to her first volume on Chicago, "I have tried to pay quite as much attention to the activities of the common man who, more or less successfully, left indelible, but frequently impersonal, traces of his contribution to community development."[31] Schlesinger influenced Pierce's and McKelvey's understandings of a wider social history that looked beyond the elite urban stratum to a whole panorama of groups. Writing approvingly in 1943 of Rochesterian Jerre Mangione's novel *Mount Allegro*, about the life of a Sicilian family in northeast Rochester, McKelvey claimed that "American social historians face no more difficult fields of research than those presented by the large, unassimilated, immigrant groups which have come to play such important roles in the cultural life of the nation. Perhaps an adequate appraisal of the contributions of these groups must await the progress of careful spade work by numerous local historians." While doubting the adequacy of his own training for this work, McKelvey nevertheless highlighted its importance—and signaled the need for historians to cast a wider net for sources, including creative work like Mangione's, in order to more fully understand the diversity of their cities.[32]

Even the more capacious social histories McKelvey and Pierce worked hard to write were, however, blinkered in their own ways. For what constitutes a complete or comprehensive urban history is a choice the writer of that history must make, rather than something somehow embedded in the material itself. As the urban historian Eric Lampard noted in 1961, "the variant 'facts of history' cannot be defined nor their significance appraised until they are treated in relation to larger conceptual frameworks."[33] The domain of all facts about a city cannot be set by those facts themselves; it must be determined by the historian, according to some "conceptual framework," as Lampard put it. The necessity for that choice is vividly present in the simple question: When does the history of a city begin? McKelvey noted the geological history of the Genesee Valley, while Pierce described the "subject treated" in her first volume as "the beginning of organized community life," which she conceptualized as "the period from the coming of the first white men (1673)."[34] A problem with the completist approach, therefore, is that its exemplary texts lack an argument for their particular version of "complete." From the perspective of Indigenous people, for example, Pierce's starting point was not an instance of historical completeness but, rather, one of historical erasure.

If the meaning of "complete" shifts away from "exhaustive," however, new possibilities appear. Complete may mean whole, as opposed to fragmentary or sundered. In 1945, the *Democrat & Chronicle* covered the publication of the first of McKelvey's four volumes. "The alert, personable historian recently discovered that his favorite hobby could be of valuable aid to him in his project. By painting downtown Rochester, using a composite of old drawings, he was able to visualize the whole civic scene instead of merely describing different social, economic or political events in the early life of Rochester."[35] When the third volume of his history was released in 1957, McKelvey used the metaphor of a puzzle to describe his work. "A community like Rochester is a microcosm—a little world with its own symbols of politics, religion, art, education," he told the *Democrat & Chronicle*. "Putting these pieces together to make a unified picture is like assembling a jigsaw puzzle. It's a job that takes time—but the results are worth it."[36] Both the painting and the puzzle comparisons are compelling ways to consider McKelvey's work.

The pieces of a jigsaw puzzle may at first appear to be a jumble of unconnected bits, but a piece is always a piece *of something*—usually, in the case of a puzzle, the image on the box top. Every brush stroke on a canvas, similarly, is a contribution to the final painting. Before McKelvey's generation of urban historians, writing about cities had often been a jumble, a collection of facts or details without an overarching story or theme or framework to bring them together. McKelvey rejected this mode of urban history, calling for "critical standards" by which masses of otherwise disparate parts might be organized into coherent wholes. He was not trying to prove an academic thesis, but McKelvey did aim to create a meaningful—the term most often used today might be "curated"—narrative. "Vast stores of daily records must be sifted," he wrote, "and the significant separated from the purely antiquarian details."[37]

Identifying the "significant" facts was no easy or straightforward task, however. In her assessment of urban biography, Green suggested that "to give to that multiple entity, a city, recognizable individuality, physical, intellectual, and spiritual, and to show why it took that particular form requires the consummate art of a portrait painter." She might have been pleased to know that McKelvey literally painted Rochester's portrait, but his third volume on Rochester she found less a portrait than "at its best . . . the work of a photographer": snapshots of disconnected moments. "At its worst," McKelvey's volume was "a scrapbook filled with old clippings and theater stubs without significance except for the one-time participants in long-past events."[38]

McKelvey's task was particularly challenging because the two concepts of complete—exhaustive and whole—pulled the urban biographer in different directions. The exhaustive urban biographer aimed to review the full extent of available sources in order to write a history that embraced the widest range of a city's people, not just its elites. The urban biographer setting out to tell the whole history of a city was obliged to weld many and disparate facts into a coherent, unified story, a process that inevitably involved a winnowing of items based on an appraisal of their significance—a significance defined with respect to the emphases the biographer had in mind. The one aim pointed toward an opening up, the other toward an attempt to pin down. McKelvey hoped to reconcile these aims, providing an exhaustive history of Rochester that also formed a unitary whole. "To be more than a chronicler," he wrote, "one must offer a synthesizing interpretation with the hope that it is sufficiently inclusive and causally meaningful to prove evocative to most readers and not too disappointing to the rest."[39] As one appreciative reviewer put it, "McKelvey has so well assimilated his tremendous research that he sees the city as a whole."[40]

The metaphors of the portrait painter and the biographer suggest an ability on the part of the artist or writer to capture the essence or character of their subject. "The object has been to use only those details, events, and personalities which help to fill in the essential features of the community pattern and to move the story along," McKelvey wrote in the foreword to his first volume.[41] But how did he—or any portraitist or biographer—determine what an "essential feature" was? "Few readers . . . will be surprised to learn," McKelvey wrote, "that my analysis has relied more on an intuitive interpretation of the available records than on a quantitative abstraction of their essence."[42] The process of intuiting the essence of a city is ultimately a black box; it is a matter of instincts rather than of analysis. While artists and writers have been praised for their intuitive abilities, historians—especially in the time of intense professionalization of the field that spanned McKelvey's career— typically were not. As one characteristic journal article from 1979 put it, "One should always be wary of impressionistic demonstrations," as opposed to "more systematic analysis."[43]

And so McKelvey hedged. "I have sometimes likened my work to that of an urban biographer," he wrote in 1962, the year after publishing the final volume of his series, "but I hope this term conveys no teleological or animistic allusions. I have tried in each volume to relate the varied developments of the period to a dominant theme that seemed to offer the most inclusive and meaningful interpretation of the multiplicity of facts that diligent research has brought to light."[44] The "dominant theme" he identified for each period corresponded to the titles of his four volumes.

> We have, in the first volume, witnessed the birth of the Genesee mill-town and its development, spurred by the opening of the Erie Canal, into a thriving "Water-Power City." In the second volume we saw that early Flour City transformed, by successive waves of immigrants, into a cosmopolitan "Flower City." The third, reviewed the joint efforts of enterprising industrialists, skilled workers, civic reformers, and social idealists, inspired by a "Quest for Quality," to transform the community again into a prosperous technological city. In this last book I have carried Rochester's story forward to the present, viewing the city as an "Emerging Metropolis."[45]

It is a revealing and laudable indication of McKelvey's commitment to not only marking but also celebrating diverse cultural "contributions," as he called them, that his second volume was less about the nursery industry in Rochester than it was about the flowering of the city's population, as newcomers from distant points arrived and made Rochester their home. His thematic foci could be inclusive in this way while reductive or exclusive in others.

Reviewers of McKelvey's four-volume *Rochester* have diverged sharply on the question of whether he had produced something exhaustive, whole, both, or neither. David Ellis, a historian at Hamilton College in Clinton, New York, reviewed McKelvey's first two volumes, finding them rewarding as well as comprehensive. "The dense foliage of detail gathered from newspapers, manuscripts, municipal records, and travel accounts is skillfully blended into a panoramic account of the city's development," he wrote of the first volume. The second, Ellis noted, "succeeded on the whole in avoiding the pitfall of overwhelming the reader with great masses of disparate detail."[46]

McKelvey's third volume, however, Constance Green judged as revealing "with disheartening clarity the difficulty of writing a well-proportioned, discerning, and readable 'biography' of a city." As Rochester expanded and became an industrial city over time, its story grew dramatically more complex. "To tell this later story effectively, with the details to establish the hows and the clarifications that furnish the whys, is necessarily a Herculean and delicate task," and McKelvey's volume "fails to leave the reader with an understanding of what sort of personality Rochester developed between 1890 and 1925." Instead, it provided "an indigestible potpourri that leaves the reader stuffed but unsatisfied. Perhaps the author's official position as city historian put subtle pressures upon him to omit nothing," Green speculated. The city biography had "again defeated the American urban historian," she concluded.[47]

Bayrd Still, who might be considered a friendly reviewer, found McKelvey's fourth and final volume exhaustive but, precisely by virtue of that, not a coherent whole. "His concern for detail and completeness of coverage gives rise, unhappily, to a profusion of facts and names which sometimes obscures the main lines of development and stands in the way of the most effective interpretive emphasis. According to information supplied on the dust jacket more than a thousand residents are mentioned in the text. This seems excessive."[48] A reviewer even of the one-book summary of Rochester history McKelvey published in 1973 found himself "bombarded with too many names, dates, places and various trivia," which "for a generalized introductory survey . . . is a little overdone."[49] Shortly after his fourth volume came out, McKelvey responded that it was "not a Who's Who of Rochester, as one commentator mistakenly described it; nor is it a compendium of all major community events." It was, he insisted, simply the continuation "in narrative form [of] my account of the city's history."[50]

Yet many readers evidently found McKelvey's work, especially when it addressed the more recent past of Rochester, too exhaustive to provide a discernable narrative: a historical account comprehensive yet not whole—an incomplete mode of completism. McKelvey's four-volume history of Rochester was both a singular achievement in urban history and a testament to the tradeoffs and difficulties of balancing the many imperatives of such work. One imperative—perhaps the overriding one for McKelvey—was to produce Rochester history that would serve Rochesterians. His work offers a vital standpoint from which to ask what such history means.

****

In 1976, *Blake McKelvey's Rochester* was first broadcast on WXXI television. As then–City Historian Joseph Barnes put it, the filmmakers faced "the extremely difficult job of compressing the history of Rochester and its region into a one-hour film." McKelvey was "the film's co-author and on-screen 'talent.'" The voiceover narration introducing him to viewers explained that McKelvey had for four decades studied Rochester history, and "one purpose of his effort has been to show that what came before explains where we are today, and that what we do today will determine the shape of tomorrow."[51]

Blake McKelvey's Rochester signaled two important ways of making his historical research better serve Rochesterians. Without giving up the aim of a complete history of the city, McKelvey had shifted from the four-volume history, finished in 1961, to the one-volume summary, published in 1973, to the one-hour film version, aired in 1976. To serve Rochesterians, McKelvey's work had to be accessible to them, and the film was the culmination of efforts to reduce barriers in terms of the medium (visual), the time commitment (one hour), and the cost (free, via public television).

Second, McKelvey sought to enliven Rochesterians with the idea that the future of their city would be determined by their present actions. As Barnes put it, the filmmakers wanted to show "that present decisions will influence the community's future just as past decisions shaped Rochester's present." Rochester's history would serve as a kind of proof for this claim, and that proof was linked to McKelvey's less empirical, more ringing statement of the case in the film's final moments: "Today and tomorrow, as in the past, we the people comprise Rochester's principal resource. We have the votes and the voices—we have the talents and the aspirations that can, and in fact do determine the breadth of participation, the vitality and warmth, indeed the very quality of life in Rochester."[52] At a fundamental level, this message told Rochesterians that the timeline of their city was continuous—the past not sealed off from the present, nor from the future. Instead, Rochesterians were living in an urban and regional environment shaped by ongoing historical processes over which they might exert some influence. As recently as 2021, an important essay attempting to revive and reorient the practice of urban biography warned against precisely the tendency that McKelvey, with his focus on city residents as agents, had decades earlier sought to overcome. Urban biography too often fostered a "dissociation between urban history, which is closed and thus ready for contemplation, and contemporary urban problems," Jaroslav Ira, a history professor at Charles University in Prague, wrote in the journal *Urban History*. "Readers are taught to be mere spectators of urban history, and not its agents."[53] Time and again, McKelvey had tried to steer away from

Blake McKelvey (top right) and members of the *Blake McKelvey's Rochester* film crew at the Genesee Country Village & Museum. *From* Rochester History *38, no. 1 (January 1976).*

this model. "As the city enters the nation's bicentennial year we return to the question with which we started," he said in the 1976 film's closing segment: "What kind of city is Rochester?"[54] The answer, McKelvey's work suggested to Rochesterians, was up to them.

McKelvey increasingly emphasized access and agency alongside his comprehensive approach to Rochester history, his efforts raising the question of what content he was making accessible and how it best served the agents he hoped to activate. Rochester history might not only make Rochesterians more aware of their formative role in the city, but also better able to play it. "A socially relevant urban biography . . . motivates readers to participate in urban issues," Ira wrote, and it equips them with "critical and applicable knowledge about the city" in order to do so more effectively.[55] As the architecture and landscape historian Kathryn E. Holliday put it in the *Journal of Urban History*, "The city biography clarifies public dialogue about the recent past and informs policy making for the future."[56]

One means of clarification is to bust myths or at least to provide counterpoints to conventional wisdom. McKelvey, in his fourth volume on Rochester, for example, pointed out that "although Rochester won the first World Brotherhood Award in June 1958, it could not hide some shameful shortcomings," particularly "the ugly fact of [racial] segregation" in the city, where "a state survey found a greater reluctance to sell to Negroes in some of Rochester's 'better neighborhoods' than in any city in the state." At other moments, however, McKelvey returned to a formulation that personified Rochester—a pitfall of urban "biography" that suggests a false analogy between an individual life and a complex, multifarious city. "Awaking at last to its responsibilities," he wrote, "Rochester began with hesitation, and then with greater assurance, to suppress its discriminatory impulse."[57] Such a sentence creates the impression of smooth consensus where there was, in fact, deep conflict. It also clearly identifies "Rochester" with white Rochesterians—for surely it was not Black Rochesterians who had a "discriminatory impulse" against themselves! Michael Frisch, a historian at the University at Buffalo and one of the key theorists of oral and public history, has pointed out that "the task of narrative urban biography has traditionally pulled authors . . . towards evocation of an anthropomorphized fictive community that can be said to act, will, think, and feel. In the past, this was usually effected by making the overall community virtually synonymous with its leading citizens and businessmen, whose personalities, activities, perspectives, and interests could be described concretely, giving focus and direction to the broader personalization of 'the city.'"[58] One major problem with such a univocal narrative was that it erased the multivocal reality of the city—the very debates that were at the heart of civic agency, which McKelvey wanted to champion.

Responding to critics of his fourth volume, McKelvey noted one who objected to "the lack of any reference to *The Voice*," which McKelvey characterized as "a struggling weekly."[59] *The Voice*, alternatively *The Frederick Douglass Voice*, was founded in 1933 by Howard W. Coles, a real-estate agent who also "produced the first survey of African American housing conditions in New York State" and was "Rochester's first African American radio announcer."[60] It was precisely the kind of source McKelvey might have quoted or otherwise drawn upon to furnish a dissenting perspective on residential segregation and housing discrimination. Too often, in the marked absence of quotations, the detached voice of the historian in McKelvey's writing papers over conflicts that might better be expressed in "the voice" of Rochesterians themselves.

Presenting a multitude of voices in a historical text is also a way of modeling the contested, ultimately deliberative public sphere of urban democracy. Ira argues that "socially relevant urban biography emulates deliberation by performing the intra-textual exchange of multiple perspectives and stimulates real debate by suggesting themes for discussion and presenting the city's past and present as a political issue."[61] Beyond Holliday's view that city biographies reanimate "the recent past," McKelvey's work suggests that the more distant past can also help frame contemporary political debates.

Consider, for example, the theme of McKelvey's first volume: Rochester as a "water-power city." He had in mind the use of the Genesee falls to power mills and the Erie Canal to conduct trade, both powerful influences on the community's early history, but the role of water is also a live civic question today. According to the City of Rochester, the contemporary "ROC the Riverway" initiative "consolidates more than two dozen transformational projects along the Genesee River into a unified strategy. This will enable Rochester to better leverage the value of its riverfront."[62] The transformations in question, however, are hotly debated.[63] Added to these contemporary debates about the role of the Genesee are those about the other major body of water to have shaped Rochester's history: Lake Ontario. In the last two decades, the lake has been a focal point for controversies surrounding public policy and the region's future, from the fate of the *Spirit of Ontario* fast ferry to Toronto, to "Plan 2014" regulating the outflow of water from the lake through the St. Lawrence, to the possibility of an influx of "climate refugees" seeking proximity to reliable sources of fresh water.[64]

McKelvey's work demonstrates that debates about water resources (and hazards) have been central to the existence and development of Rochester. The relationship between public policy and nature has been a vivid part of the city's history from the beginning. Amid the Napoleonic wars and President Thomas Jefferson's policy response to them, trade "was suddenly checked when the Embargo and Non-Intercourse Acts stopped exports and glutted the Atlantic markets after 1808," McKelvey wrote. The Lake Ontario border with British Canada, however, was a porous one, and commerce across the lake continued even as other routes closed. "Several enterprising villages quickly appeared" along the lower Genesee to seize this opportunity, McKelvey noted, "though the contest for priority [among them] which ensued was not to be terminated until the hazards of a frontier war and the charting of a new trade artery gave advantage to Rochester." The War of 1812 and the building of the Erie Canal made Rochester the urban center of the Genesee, but before those political events determined, literally and figuratively, the course of regional waterways, there were multiple potential directions for the development of the area as, McKelvey observed, either "a bridgehead, a mill town, or a lake port"—all of them contingent upon orientations to water, as obstacle, resource, or thoroughfare.[65] As Rochesterians debate competing visions for the use of water resources today, they may find in the early history of the city a precedent for a highly political process in which there were clashing interests, winners, and losers. Such urban biography is bracing when it helps contemporary people realize that the processes shaping their city are not inevitable but, rather, in their hands—the very message that McKelvey highlighted, time and again.

This approach to urban biography, one that activates the agency of and provides vital information to city residents, casts new light on the question of what a "complete" city history means. From an academic perspective, defining the complete history of a thing resembles the question of how many angels fit on the head of a pin—it is abstract. A pragmatist's approach, by contrast, asks: Complete with respect to what purpose? A complete history is, from this point of view, a serviceable one. If the purpose of accessible (as opposed to strictly academic) city histories is to best equip city residents for civic life, then a complete history is one that fully serves that aim. Since the present continuously raises new questions for the past, and since the needs of city residents will continue changing, the pragmatic version of a "complete" city history will have to regularly change as well. What is serviceable in one moment may not be in another.

In the years since McKelvey published his fourth volume in 1961, new books on Rochester history have both addressed the decades after that date and emphasized the centrality of a concern too peripheral to McKelvey's original quartet: race relations in Rochester. They include Lou Buttino and Mark Hare's *The Remaking of a City: Rochester, NY, 1964–1984* (1984), Laura Warren Hill's, *Strike the Hammer: The Black Freedom Struggle in Rochester, New York, 1940–1970* (2021), and Justin Murphy's *Your Children Are Very Greatly in Danger: School Segregation in Rochester, New York* (2022). The model of a completist approach to city history as presented by Bessie Louise Pierce and

Blake McKelvey is that of one mind struggling to get hold of an entire body of information. Even when Pierce employed teams of research assistants, the young McKelvey among them, it was ultimately she who had to assimilate all their findings and fashion a complete narrative. An apt metaphor for this model is McKelvey's custom of climbing hills to get as complete a view of a city as possible. "I can well remember my first view of Rochester . . . from the top of Cobbs Hill," he said in *Blake McKelvey's Rochester*. "I recall my impression of the city, in the summer of 1936, as a tranquil, homeowner's town, spreading out under a green canopy. Only the Kodak Tower, scattered chimneys and steeples were visible above the tree tops."[66]

The project of a complete city history, however, is not that of a single climber scaling a mound of research to get an above-the-tree-line view. Rather than a completist history, the people of a city complete its history as they look to the past with new concerns and discover in that process both what existing histories of their city offer and how they fall short, prompting new research and raising new questions. As McKelvey understood, historians' "omissions may prove so important that" their "interpretation is discredited. Later events, too, may take a direction that prompts a restudy of the entire period."[67] The "big flaw" with urban "biography," the writer Scott Martelle—a Rochester resident but an urban biographer of Detroit—observes, "is that a life ends, and a city (usually) does not."[68] As the history of Rochester or any city continues, so must the process of understanding its past in light of its unfolding present. "The historian can never feel sure that his account will stand the test of time," McKelvey wrote, "but if his insights provide a measure of self-awareness and understanding to his generation, they will, no doubt, raise up successors who will take care of the future."[69] A complete history is always one in the making, the work not of one mind but of many.

Acknowledgments
I would like to thank the *Rochester History* team—folks from RIT and from the Office of the City Historian—for their assistance with this article and their work on the journal. I am thankful to Anne Cook for her edits and to Rich Newman and Justin Murphy for their helpful comments on earlier versions of this article. Scott Martelle kindly shared his thoughts on urban biography with me. ■

1. Biographical content from Bruce M. Stave, "A Conversation with Blake McKelvey," *Journal of Urban History* 2, no. 4 (August 1976): 459–86.

2. Stave, "Conversation with McKelvey," 459–60.

3. Blake McKelvey, "The Voice of the City Historian," *Rochester History* 51, no. 1 (Winter 1989): 17.

4. Stave to McKelvey in 1976: "You are well known for several books, but very well known for the four-volume study of Rochester, an urban biography." Stave, "Conversation with McKelvey," 470.

5. Bruce M. Stave, "A Conversation with Bayrd Still," *Journal of Urban History* 3, no. 3 (May 1977): 337.

6. Stave, "Conversation with Still," 337.

7. McKelvey had completed his PhD in 1933, then worked at a New Deal survey of historical documents in Pennsylvania before going to Chicago. On the circumstances of McKelvey's position in Chicago, see Bessie Louise Pierce to Blake McKelvey, June 1, 1934, Bessie Louise Pierce Papers [Box 13, Folder 7], Hanna Holborn Gray Special Collections Research Center, University of Chicago Library.

8. Richard Hofstadter characterized the Progressive historians as "eager to make up for the past failure of historians to deal with the interests of the common man and with the historic merits of movements of reform. They attempted to find a usable past related to the broadest needs of a nation fully launched upon its own industrialization, and to make history an active instrument of self-recognition and self-improvement." Hofstadter, *The Progressive Historians: Turner, Beard, Parrington* (University of Chicago Press Phoenix Edition, 1979; orig. 1968), xvi–xvii. Though Hofstadter wrote about scholars older than McKelvey, Arthur M. Schlesinger Sr., who advised Pierce and McKelvey when they were graduate students, had studied with Charles Beard, one of the signal Progressive historians, at Columbia and had succeeded Frederick Jackson Turner, another, at Harvard.

9. Biographical Note, Guide to the Bessie Louise Pierce Papers 1839–1974; Hanna Holborn Gray Special Collections Research Center at the University of Chicago Library, 2006, https://www.lib.uchicago.edu/e/scrc/findingaids/view.php?eadid=ICU.SPCL.PIERCE#idp3348168.

10. McKelvey, "Voice of the City Historian," *Rochester History* 51, no. 1 (Winter 1989): 17.

11. Paul D. Evans, review of *Rochester: The Flower City, 1855–1890* by Blake McKelvey, *The Mississippi Valley Historical Review* 36, no. 4 (March 1950): 702.

12. Theodore Hershberg, "The New Urban History: Toward an Interdisciplinary History of the City," *Journal of Urban History* 5, no. 1 (November 1978): 4–5.

13. Blake McKelvey, *Rochester: The Water-Power City, 1812–1854* (Harvard University Press, 1945), ix; Dexter Perkins, preface to McKelvey, *Rochester: The Water-Power City, 1812–1854*, v; front matter. On Gleason, see Michael J. Brown, Rebecca A. R. Edwards, and Tina Olsin Lent, "Kate Gleason: Introducing a Twentieth-Century Businesswoman to Twenty-First Century Students," *Seneca Falls Dialogues Journal* 2 (Fall 2017): 1–23.

14. Stave, "Conversation with McKelvey," 471.

15. Blake McKelvey, "Errata and Addenda, Plus Some Thoughts on the Nature of History and the Rochester Story," *Rochester History* 24, no. 2 (April 1962): 22.

16. McKelvey, "Errata and Addenda," 22.

17. Blake McKelvey, *Rochester on the Genesee: The Growth of a City*, 2nd ed. (Syracuse University Press, 1993), xiv, 316.

18. Biographical Note, Guide to the Bessie Louise Pierce Papers 1839—1974; Hanna Holborn Gray Special Collections Research Center at the University of Chicago Library, 2006, https://www.lib.uchicago.edu/e/scrc/findingaids/view.php?eadid=ICU.SPCL.PIERCE#idp3348168.

19. Stave, "Conversation with McKelvey," 465–66, 470.

20. Biographical Note, Guide to the Bessie Louise Pierce Papers 1839–1974; Hanna Holborn Gray Special Collections Research Center at the University of Chicago Library, 2006, https://www.lib.uchicago.edu/e/scrc/findingaids/view.php?eadid=ICU.SPCL.PIERCE#idp3348168.

21. Pero Gaglo Dagbovie, "Black Women Historians from the Late 19th Century to the Dawning of the Civil Rights Movement," *The Journal of African American History* 89, no. 3 (Summer 2004): 254; Felicia D. Render, "An Afro-American's Quest for Education: The Elsie M. Lewis papers," Amistad Research Center, https://www.amistadresearchcenter.org/single-post/elsie-m-lewis-papers.

22. Bessie Louise Pierce to Elsie Lewis Makel, May 20, 1954, Bessie Louise Pierce Papers [Box 13, Folder 7], Hanna Holborn Gray Special Collections Research Center, University of Chicago Library.

23. Blake McKelvey, "A City Historian's Report," *Rochester History* 35, no. 3 (July 1973): 7.

24. Stave, "Conversation with McKelvey," 472.

25. Stave, "Conversation with Still," 337–38.

26. Deborah Fineblum Raub, "His Story," *Democrat & Chronicle*, December 14, 1999, C1.

27. Estelle F. Feinstein, review of *Rochester on the Genesee: The Growth of a City* by Blake McKelvey, *Journal of American History* 61, no. 3 (December 1974): 804.

28. Constance McLaughlin Greene, "The Value of Local History," in *The Cultural Approach to History*, ed. Caroline F. Ware (Columbia University Press, 1940), 275.

29. Arthur M. Schlesinger, *In Retrospect: The History of a Historian* (Harcourt Brace, 1963), 99.

30. Bessie Louise Pierce, *A History of Chicago Volume 1: The Beginning of a City, 1673-1848* (University of Chicago Press, 1937, reprint 1975), xvii; Blake McKelvey, *Rochester: The Water-Power City, 1812-1854* (Harvard University Press, 1945), xi.

31. Pierce, *History of Chicago Volume 1*, xvi.

32. Blake McKelvey, review of *Mount Allegro* by Jerre Mangione, illustrated by Peggy Bacon, *New York History* 24, no. 4 (October 1943): 580.

33. Eric E. Lampard, "American Historians and the Study of Urbanization," *American Historical Review* 67, no. 1 (October 1961): 54.

34. Pierce, *History of Chicago Volume 1*, xv.

35. "Second Historical Volume Started as First Appears," *Democrat & Chronicle*, October 9, 1945, 14. Two of McKelvey's paintings were selected for the Annual Finger Lakes Exhibition that year.

36. Constance Gomperts, "Past's Puzzle No Problem," *Democrat & Chronicle*, May 5, 1957, C1.

37. Blake McKelvey, "American Urban History Today," *American Historical Review* 57, no. 4 (July 1952): 919–20.

38. Constance McLaughlin Green, review of *Rochester, The Quest for Quality, 1890-1925* by Blake McKelvey, *Journal of Economic History* 17, no. 2 (June 1957): 303.

39. McKelvey, "Errata and Addenda," 5.

40. William E. Rowley, review of *Rochester: The Quest for Quality, 1890-1925* by Blake McKelvey, *Wisconsin Magazine of History* 41, no. 1 (Autumn 1957): 69.

41. McKelvey, *Rochester: Water-Power City*, vii.

42. McKelvey, "City Historian's Report," 1.

43. Michael Hechter, "On Separatism and Ethnicity: A Response to Sloan's 'Ethnicity or Imperialism?'" *Comparative Studies in Society and History* 21, no. 1 (1979): 127.

44. McKelvey, "Errata and Addenda," 6.

45. Blake McKelvey, *Rochester: An Emerging Metropolis, 1925-1961* (Christopher Press, 1961), v.

46. David M. Ellis, review of *Rochester: The Water-Power City, 1812-1854* by McKelvey, *Mississippi Valley Historical Review* 32, no. 4 (March 1946): 607; Ellis, review of *Rochester, The Flower City, 1855-1890* by McKelvey, *New York History* 31, no. 1 (January 1950): 84. Ellis was well positioned to comment on these aspects of McKelvey's work, for students at Hamilton "who took his course could expect plenty of names and dates, plenty of details. These details [were] spooled out to the class in a way that gave him the nickname 'Spooly.'" Jay Williams, "David Ellis '38," Faculty Memorial Minutes, 4 May 1999, https://www.hamilton.edu/about/history/memorial-minutes/david-ellis.

47. Constance McLaughlin Green, review of *Rochester, The Quest for Quality*, 302–3.

48. Bayrd Still, review of *Rochester: An Emerging Metropolis, 1925–1961* by Blake McKelvey, *Mississippi Valley Historical Review* 49, no. 2 (September 1962): 360.

49. Robert J. Wechman, review of *Rochester on the Genesee: The Growth of a City* by Blake McKelvey, *New York History* 55, no. 3 (July 1974): 339.

50. McKelvey, "Errata and Addenda," 10.

51. Joseph W. Barnes, foreword to "'Blake McKelvey's Rochester' Script from a One-Hour Film Documentary," *Rochester History* 38, no. 1 (January 1976): 1–2; McKelvey and Barnes, "'Blake McKelvey's Rochester' Script from a One-Hour Film Documentary," 5.

52. Barnes, foreword to "'McKelvey's Rochester' Script," 2; McKelvey and Barnes, "'McKelvey's Rochester' Script," 24.

53. Jaroslav Ira, "Rethinking the Genre: Urban Biographies as Means of Creating Critical Public Spheres," *Urban History* 48, no. 1 (2021): https://doi.org/10.1017/S0963926819001123.

54. McKelvey and Barnes, "'McKelvey's Rochester' Script," 24.

55. Ira, "Rethinking."

56. Kathryn E. Holliday, "Place and the City Biography: Between the Local and the Universal in the Sun Belt," *Journal of Urban History* 40, no. 4 (2014): 794.

57. McKelvey, *Rochester: An Emerging Metropolis*, 336–37.

58. Michael H. Frisch, "Get the Picture? A Review Essay," *New York History* 69, no. 2 (April 1988): 193–94.

59. In response, McKelvey indicated that he "did take note" of *The Voice* "in an article on local Negro history." The substance of the criticism, however, was that McKelvey ought to have used this source to inform his book on the city's overall history. McKelvey, "Errata and Addenda," 17.

60. Rochester Voices, "Interview, Howard Coles," from the collections of the Local History & Genealogy Division of the Rochester Public Library, https://www.rochestervoices.org/historical-media/interview-howard-coles/.

61. Ira, "Rethinking."

62. City of Rochester, "ROC the Riverway," accessed December 1, 2024, https://www.cityofrochester.gov/departments/department-environmental-services/roc-riverway.

63. For recent coverage of varied visions for the urban river corridor, particularly the future of the Broad Street crossing, see Amorette Miller, "Rochester's Historical Aqueduct Will Be Repurposed. What Will Happen to the Graffiti Art?" *Democrat & Chronicle*, July 28, 2022, https://www.democratandchronicle.com/story/lifestyle/2022/07/28/rochester-abandoned-subway-roc-the-riverway-renovation-graffiti-art-future/65380568007/.

64. A sampling of the extensive reporting on the ferry, lake levels, and climate impacts includes: "Flawed Business Plan Sank Fast Ferry," *Rochester Business Journal*, July 4, 2014, https://rbj.net/2014/; Jacob Schermerhorn, "Revisiting Plan 2014," *Rochester Beacon*, April 21, 2022, https://rochesterbeacon.com/2022/04/21/revisiting-plan-2014/; and Clare Boegel, "Are We Ready to be a Climate Refuge?" *Rochester Beacon*, April 27, 2023, https://rochesterbeacon.com/2023/04/27/are-we-ready-to-be-a-climate-refuge/.

65. McKelvey, *Rochester: The Water-Power City*," 29–30.

66. McKelvey and Barnes, "'Blake McKelvey's Rochester' Script," 5.

67. McKelvey, "Errata and Addenda," 5.

68. Scott Martelle, email to the author, November 19, 2024.

69. McKelvey, "Errata and Addenda," 5.

"Nature Carves a Choice Urban Site"
Revisiting Environmental Themes in Blake McKelvey's Rochester: The Water-Power City, 1812–1854

Christine Keiner

As humanity enters a new era, "the age of water insecurity," no one can ever again take water for granted—even those of us fortunate to live in the Great Lakes region. Coined by Norwegian geographer-historian Terje Tvedt in 2007, the phrase refers to the increasing frequency and severe consequences on societies worldwide of floods, droughts, waterborne diseases, aging water infrastructure, cross-border water conflicts, and other intensifying problems and uncertainties limiting access to safe water.[1] Compounded by anthropogenic (that is, human-caused) climate changes to the hydrologic cycle, water crises are forcing people to pay more attention to the quality and quantity of the water upon which they rely—in other words, to wake up from the "age of general waterblindness" [*sic*] that has characterized modernity.[2]

Historians and allied scholars in the humanities and social sciences have important roles to play in educating the public and politicians about the centrality of water to social development, and yet even they have a long record of "water blindness." The field of environmental history, which arose during the 1970s in partial response to the complex environmental issues of the day, focused heavily until the early 2000s on land-based places and problems.[3] At long last, environmental historians and other scholars are helping us rethink relationships between humans and watery environments by producing exciting books and articles that historicize the planet's oceans, bays, lakes, and rivers.[4] Such works analyze waterways as active forces, rather than "as merely the backdrop against which human history unfolded."[5]

Christine Keiner is the author of *The Oyster Question: Scientists, Watermen, and the Maryland Chesapeake since 1880* and *Deep Cut: Science, Power, and the Unbuilt Interoceanic Canal.* She is the chair of the Department of Science, Technology, and Society at Rochester Institute of Technology.

A circa 1856 engraving of a panoramic view of Rochester and the Genesee River, looking north. The engraving was made from a lithograph by English artist Edwin Whitefield, who did several panoramic views of cities in New York. *From the Collection of the Rochester Public Library Local History & Genealogy Division.*

That is not to say that no one recognized the dynamic roles of aquatic eco-systems in urban contexts in previous eras—which brings us to Blake McKelvey and his 1945 book, *Rochester: The Water-Power City, 1812–1854*. The first of four volumes encompassing the early 1800s to 1961, it was written by McKelvey long before the rise of environmental history and other historical subfields that directed attention away from political elites toward a much more diverse set of human and nonhuman actors.[6] For his subtitle, he could have chosen the familiar moniker "The Flour City" to recognize the dominance of wheat milling during the city's early decades. However, by emphasizing waterpower, McKelvey evoked a broader sense of nature's role in Rochester's rise to prominence.

As discussed in this special issue by historians Michael Brown and Christine L. Ridarsky, McKelvey graduated from Harvard University with a PhD in history and worked as a research assistant for University of Chicago historian Bessie Louise Pierce on her groundbreaking set of volumes, *A History of Chicago*.[7] Soon thereafter, McKelvey began researching his own urban project during the late 1930s as the assistant city historian of Rochester, New York. As his boss, City Historian Dexter Perkins, explained in the preface of *Rochester: The Water-Power City*, New York State law required towns and cities to appoint their own historians as civil servants. The book thus signified something unusual: "The present volume represents if not a unique, at any rate a most striking, achievement, the preparation of a history of an important American city on the basis of careful research, exact scholarship, and expert judgment all provided for by municipal funds."[8] Moreover, Perkins praised his colleague for his expansive perspective: "His book deserves to be read not only by those who are interested in Rochester, but also by those who are interested in the growth of urban living in America."[9]

Indeed, although McKelvey chose "The Water-Power City" as his subtitle (emphasis added), Rochester's early reliance upon riverine energy was a common, longstanding feature of dense settlements around the globe. McKelvey's advisor at Harvard, Arthur M. Schlesinger, in his influential 1940 article "The City in American History," made this clear with respect to early nineteenth-century North America. While massive numbers of migrants were moving westward (and attracting the bulk of attention from later generations of historians), "in the East, scores of new cities sprang into being, generally at the fall line of the rivers, where waterpower was available for utilizing the industrial secrets which sharp-witted Americans had recently filched from Britain."[10] Rochester was one of many antebellum "water-power cities," but few urban or environmental historians of the twentieth century used such a framing concept. Not until the 1990s and early 2000s, respectively, did urban environmental history and urban river studies emerge as distinctive fields of inquiry.[11]

As part of this eightieth-anniversary forum, I am delighted to have the opportunity to explore McKelvey's approach to urban environmental themes in *Rochester: The Water-Power City, 1812–1854*, to address some relevant recent scholarship, and to suggest future studies that build upon McKelvey's foundation. McKelvey deserves attention for transcending the "water blindness" prevalent among so many historians for so long.

I also want to highlight other stories of urban nature-society relationships sprinkled throughout his text. While the hydropower furnished by the Genesee River for flour production is the dominant environmental (not to mention capitalist) dimension in McKelvey's narrative, it is not the only one. Urban living, after all, entails numerous kinds of interactions between nature and society, and the beginning period of a city's emergence from so-called wilderness presents multiple points of contact and conflict not only between different groups of people, but also between human and nonhuman organisms and entities.

A fruitful set of approaches and questions for addressing urban environmental themes comes from a provocative 1994 article by Christine Meisner Rosen and Joel Tarr. In their introduction to a special issue of the *Journal of Urban History*, "The Environment and the City," they argued that "urban historians have as much to contribute to society's understanding of the environmental evolution of the earth as do historians of agriculture and wilderness. Rather than

An early twentieth-century postcard depicting the Genesee River. The river, which flows from Potter County, Pennsylvania, to Lake Ontario in Rochester, New York, derives its name from a Seneca word commonly interpreted to mean "pleasant valley." *From the Collection of the Rochester Public Library Local History & Genealogy Division.*

distract attention from the history of society's transformation of the natural environment, the urban perspective contributes to the historical understanding of that transformation." To that end, Rosen and Tarr identified four major themes for elucidating historical relationships between people and nature in the context of cities: analyzing how the natural/biophysical environment affects cities; analyzing how urban communities impact natural environments over time; studying societal responses to urban impacts and initiatives to solve environmental problems; and examining the built environment and "its role and place in human life as part of the physical context in which society evolves."[12] In the context of this short essay, selectively applying these ideas to McKelvey's book helps us think more deeply about the interdependence between nineteenth-century Rochester and its residents, the Genesee River, and the Genesee Valley hinterlands.

Effects of the Natural Environment on City Life

In the opening chapter, under the section titled "Nature Carves a Choice Urban Site," McKelvey argues that Rochester's emergence at the Upper Falls of the Genesee River was practically predestined. He addresses the geological evolution of the Genesee River valley in ways redolent of geographical, climate, and environmental determinism—the idea that geography, climate, and other environmental features play strong roles in human and societal development. The book opens as follows: "If ever a town's site was prepared and its character largely determined by the varied actions of an ever-abundant water supply, it was the Rochester of a hundred years ago. So well was this site designed for a milling and trading center that in 1812, when permanent settlers arrived in the wake of the first great wave of westward migration across New York State, few traces of earlier habitation remained."[13]

Subsequent passages discuss the end of the last ice age, approximately 12,000 years ago.

A circa 1800 painting of the Upper Falls (now known as High Falls) by Louis Charles d'Orléans, Count of Beaujolais, brother of the French king Louis Philippe I. This is perhaps the earliest painting representing the Rochester area. *From the Collection of the Rochester Public Library Local History & Genealogy Division.*

As the glaciers melted, the ancient Genesee River carved out postglacial channels, thereby "providing ideal canoe trails for the Iroquois and early white traders and opening natural routes for the cross-state canals, railroads, and highways of a later day" and creating "a succession of waterfalls, destined finally to play a significant role in the growth of the city." McKelvey concludes the section by exclaiming, "Scarcely could a more fortunate combination of natural advantages have been assembled had an All-wise Providence set itself the task of preparing a site for Rochester!"[14]

Few, if any, historians today would adopt such an approach to analyzing landscapes of the past. At best, environmental and geographic determinism overlooks the contingent forces underlying all historical processes; at worst, determinist attitudes have a long record of supporting racism.[15] McKelvey's determinist descriptions in the first chapter suggest that the upper Genesee landscape was destined to be best utilized by a particular group of superior humans: "The experience of successive human invasions was to demonstrate that the site had been so designed as to attract only an advanced commercial and industrial settlement, such as the New England migrants of the early nineteenth century were to build." The first chapter does provide some details about the region's Native Americans, as conveyed by "three generations of diligent archeologists [who] have finally woven the scant traces of local Indian occupation into a fascinating story." However, McKelvey frames his brief discussion of the ways in which the Seneca interacted with the lands, waters, and European explorers of the Genesee Country in the demeaning context of "Local Antiquities and Clashing Empires."[16] Since the book's publication, scholarship on Native American environmental history has greatly expanded, and recent archaeological studies of Haudenosaunee villages and settlement patterns challenge problematic assumptions about historical urban development and the presumed technological superiority of the European Americans who established Rochester.[17]

Despite the book's initial focus on the ideal geological design of Rochester for harnessing waterpower on a large scale, McKelvey shifts gears in chapter two by suggesting that Rochester's development as a mill town was not actually inevitable. He addresses the competing commercial sites that sprang up nearby in the early 1800s and emphasizes the intense "contest for priority" among the "rival town sites" that emerged along the Genesee River and Irondequoit Creek.[18] McKelvey thereby leavens his geological determinism with a more illuminating view of history that emphasizes the primacy of social negotiations and decision-making processes by powerful stakeholder groups. As discussed by Michael Brown in his essay in this forum, McKelvey's later volumes highlight this theme—that the political processes and debates shaping urban development are anything but inevitable.[19]

A circa 1907-1914 postcard depicting the flour mill of C.J. Hill and Son, located on South Water Street. The mill was established in 1831 and operated until around 1875. *From the Collection of the Rochester Public Library Local History & Genealogy Division.*

Early Rochester and its rivals all depended upon river-powered mills. Gristmills ground the wheat grown by farmers in the fertile Genesee Valley into flour. Sawmills transformed the thick forests of pine, maple, ash, elm, and oak into lumber for houses, barrels, and the boats that transported flour, whiskey, pork, potash, and other commodified products of nature to distant markets via Lake Ontario, the Genesee River, and, later, the Erie Canal. By 1816, the year before its incorporation as a village, "Rochester was recognized as the principal grain market of western New York, where, despite the 'cold summer' of 1816 and the tedious labor

An illustration showing the first Erie Canal aqueduct over the Genesee River, completed in 1823. It was situated just north of the location of the 1842 Aqueduct, which later became Broad Street when the Erie Canal was rerouted from downtown Rochester. *From the Collection of the Rochester Public Library Local History & Genealogy Division.*

of plowing, harvesting and threshing, wheat was becoming a major crop."[20] Probably not incidentally, that "cold summer," as documented by subsequent historians and scientists, was a worldwide phenomenon that followed a massive volcanic eruption in Indonesia, causing crop failures and migrations of desperate people throughout the Northern Hemisphere.[21] McKelvey's note suggests the usefulness of conducting further research on the Tambora eruption's climatic and social effects on the development of the Western New York region and other human migratory movements circa 1816.

Effects of the Built Environment on the Natural Environment

The development that cemented Rochester's advantage among its rivals was the Erie Canal, or more specifically, the routing of the canal via a sandstone aqueduct across the Genesee River in Rochester. McKelvey recounts this political decision with a strong dash of environmental determinism: "To be sure, the canal act [passed by the state legislature in 1817] did not determine either the exact route or the full extent of the projected trade artery, but geology had taken care of Rochester."[22] As he explains, given the Genesee's wide flood plain, building the canal at another site to the south would have required digging a much deeper ditch through the river or building a dam with a long, high aqueduct across the Genesee Valley. Such construction works were therefore not physically impossible but would have been much more expensive and time-consuming than building an aqueduct across the river just below the Upper Falls in Rochester.

Even so, uncertainties about the canal's ultimate route, including whether the state would divert it to Oswego on Lake Ontario, did not resolve until 1821: "The letting of the contract for the Genesee aqueduct that autumn gave Rochester final assurance of the canal crossing and released the energies of many who had been awaiting that decision before developing their properties."[23]

As a large chunk of the book describes, the Erie Canal transformed the entire region. Before the canal's completion in 1825, it took fifteen to twenty days to transport "the increasingly abundant products of forest, field, and orchard" by wagon or sled from Buffalo to Albany.[24] By drastically cutting the time and costs of shipping goods overland, the canal spurred massive economic and environmental changes: "The town's growth during the twenties proved as great a surprise to the villagers themselves as to everybody else, for never before had America witnessed the phenomenon of such a town springing up almost overnight in the midst of a forest."[25] McKelvey evokes this sense of shock with an effective symbol, the forced uprooting after just a few years of Colonel Nathaniel Rochester's pear orchard to make space for new development near the Four Corners.[26]

McKelvey hints at other ecological shifts accompanying urbanization, including the draining of swamps, the digging of wells, and the construction of rudimentary streets. A Scottish visitor noted in 1831 that Rochester exemplified the "'progress of stumps to steeples.'"[27] Two decades later, one of the city's cultural amenities included a Sportsman's Club,

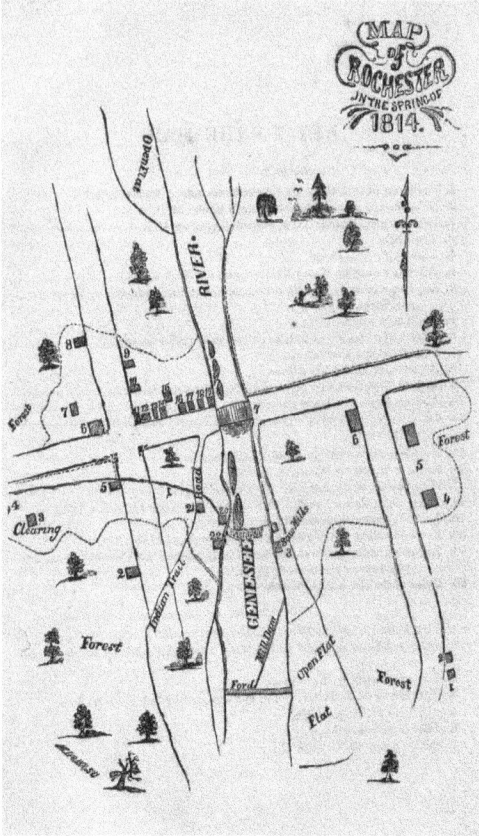

The four corners, once home to Nathaniel Rochester's pear orchards, appear on the west side of the Genesee River on this map of Rochester in the spring of 1814 created by John Kelsey in 1854. The intersection of State, Main, and Exchange Streets would form the heart of Rochester's business district for much of the nineteenth century. *From the Collection of the Rochester Public Library Local History & Genealogy Division.*

A circa 1838 illustration of the Rochester House hotel on the Erie Canal. The hotel, erected around 1827 by Palmer Cleveland, was located on the south side of the canal west of the aqueduct. It was one of many businesses that cropped up in Rochester following the canal's opening in 1825. *From the Collection of the Rochester Public Library Local History & Genealogy Division.*

whose members each shot hundreds of pigeons per day during their migrating season.[28] By this, McKelvey means the passenger pigeon, the iconic North American species driven to extinction by humans by the early twentieth century. Reflecting the former ecological richness of the Great Lakes habitat, the Rochester Museum and Science Center now contains one of the world's largest collections of passenger pigeon remains, some of which it has provided for "de-extinction" cloning studies, a topic of great scientific interest that deserves more historiographical attention.[29]

Transforming the lands surrounding the Genesee's Upper Falls into an urban site had a profound effect on the region's plant and animal life, but not on all aspects of the environment. In one of the book's curiously few references to Western New York's infamous winters (another topic about which we need more research[30]), McKelvey makes clear that the human conquest of nature was by no means immediate nor complete: "The seasons and the elements still played vital roles in the life of Rochester. Not only did the snow drifts of one season and the miry bogs of the next directly affect the general welfare, but the power-giving Genesee remained a treacherous benefactor which might at any moment snatch back the wealth and influence it had bestowed."[31] Indeed, the Genesee River of the boomtown era and beyond functioned not only as "a trade artery and power source," but also as a flood hazard that demanded respect.[32] For these reasons, early Rochesterians could not afford to indulge in water blindness.

Societal Responses to Urban Impacts and Efforts to Alleviate Environmental Problems

Enriched by the revenue generated by the Erie Canal's growing traffic, by 1834—the year of its incorporation as a city—"Rochester, the Flour City, emerged as the economic capital of a flourishing region."[33] But becoming "America's first boom town" brought complex problems, too.[34] McKelvey's analysis includes some important environmental issues that confounded the city's early leaders, especially related to floods, fires, cholera epidemics, and the lack of adequate water systems.

Of all these hazards, the one that dominates McKelvey's narrative is that of fire. Not surprisingly in a place as frigid as Rochester, at a time when "the better homes . . . boasted a fireplace in each downstairs room," each of which consumed up to ten cords of wood per winter, fires broke out frequently.[35] While civic leaders resisted spending the very limited public funds on sewers, sidewalks, and bridges, they purchased a hand pump fed by a tank and "the bucket brigade" in 1818, upgraded to a more elaborate fire engine with a 300-foot leather hose in 1827, and possessed six engines and one ladder company by 1834.[36] However, the longstanding lack of adequate water reservoirs greatly hampered fire fighters. Rochester's "civil complacency" and property owners' unwillingness to "pay the taxes necessary for a water system" fueled "waves of destructive fires" during the ensuing decades.[37] Not until 1874 did the city adopt comprehensive means of fire control; McKelvey comments in a footnote, "This was the civic field in which Rochester contrasted most unfavorably with many of its contemporaries during the fifties and sixties."[38] Given the recent emergence of scholarship examining the antebellum history of disaster politics, I hope more historians will focus on this dimension of the Flour City.[39]

Another recurring crisis that consumed Rochester during its boom years related to a different aspect of the community's rudimentary public water infra-structure—cholera. The terrifying, mysterious disease first arrived via human migrants "over the canal from the East" in July 1832. In total, 1,000 of the town's 12,000 residents fled, and 118 people died, the last in September.[40] Later that year, the board of health provided free vaccinations when smallpox hit, but when cholera roared through again in 1849, Rochester, now a city of 35,000, remained "woefully unprepared to cope with a serious epidemic."[41] When the reconvened board of health tried to build a makeshift hospital in the Eighth Ward, angry residents burned it down. Although a temporary hospital opened north of the town, where many hoped "the lake breezes would dilute the dangerous cholera vapors," the return of winter weather "dispelled fear of the plague's renewal, the hospital closed and the community slipped back into its more comfortable disregard of sanitary ordinances."[42] Three years later, another cholera outbreak spurred the health officers to begin cleaning up in April, rather than June, the sewers that had clogged over the winter. Yet once again they struggled to find a location for an emergency hospital, and "in desperation, the board requisitioned a building in the Negro quarter on High Street

High Street as featured in the 1851 Plan of the City of Rochester, N.Y. by Marcus Smith. The road was renamed Caledonia Street in 1868 before it eventually earned its current name, Clarissa Street. The historic avenue and its surrounding neighborhood have been home to an African American community since the early 1800s. *From the Collection of the Rochester Public Library Local History & Genealogy Division.*

[now Clarissa Street]."[43] This is one of the few mentions in the book of African Americans. Like many urban communities of color, Rochester's antebellum

Black population lacked the power to push back against intrusions into their neighborhood, and thus this story suggests an early case of relevance to the study of environmental racism and justice.[44]

The death toll of the 1852 cholera epidemic reached a sobering 469, prompting debate over the nature of the epidemic's severity, yet general agreement that Rochester's climatic conditions played a contributing role: "The city's peculiar situation—built for the most part on flat tableland, inclined to be swampy, with the river, canal ways, and basins providing ample surface for evaporation—created a humid atmosphere, accentuated by the spray from the falls, the evaporation from the lakes to the north and west, and finally the heavy rains which continued intermittently throughout the summer."[45] Consistent with health authorities elsewhere, the board of health also hypothesized that overcrowding in housing blocks with poor ventilation and sewer-flooded cellars allowed "'poisoned air imprisoned in the cellar beneath'" to fill the buildings with "'noxious gases.'"[46]

Perhaps because it is so famous in the history of epidemiology, McKelvey does not mention that in 1854, the English physician John Snow demonstrated that cholera spreads not through noxious vapors but rather through fecal-contaminated water.[47] Instead, McKelvey concludes his discussion of the 1852 epidemic by noting that, unlike after the previous waves of the disease, "Rochester did not return completely to its old complacent ways, for the board submitted recommendations as well as statistics, and the newly elected mayor the next spring took occasion to indorse their demand for a better sewer system."[48] Even more than fire, the 1852 cholera outbreak exposed the interdependence between the urban environment, water infrastructure, and human health.

The Co-Evolution of the Built Environment and Human Society
For Rosen and Tarr's final category, as McKelvey's narrative builds toward the terminal point of 1854, I want to address Rochester's transition from "The Flour City" to "The Flower City." During the 1840s, significant environmental and economic changes took place. In an ironic twist, the Erie Canal lowered prices enough to enable western wheat to start displacing the wheat grown in the Genesee Valley—leading farmers to diversify their crops. Due to productivity declines, hinterland growers also began relying more on fertilizers, though McKelvey does not mention whether they were based on guano (tropical seabird excrement), for which shipments commenced to the United States around 1843.[49] He does note that Upstate New Yorkers imported mulberry trees from

China to try to develop a silk industry. While that "craze" quickly fizzled out, it symbolized bigger changes on the horizon: "Though not suspected at the time, Rochester's future was to be more closely identified with its budding nursery industry, product of the Genesee Country's fertility rather than of its waterpower."[50]

Just as entrepreneurs had utilized the river to expedite flour milling and other trades requiring consistent power in the era preceding fossil fuels, so did later generations of innovators exploit regional resources to grow ornamental and fruit trees for profit. Several nurseries sprang up in fields around the city's edges by the early 1840s, led by the German Irish immigrant team of George Ellwanger and Patrick Barry. In McKelvey's breezy words, "The nursery business proved a happy find for the Flour City."[51]

A convergence of socioenvironmental forces facilitated the horticultural industry. The Erie Canal enabled commercial cultivators to ship their stock eight days ahead of Hudson Valley rivals to high-demand western markets. The northern winters, in combination with Lake Ontario's moderating climate, acclimated plants to "rigorous climates" more effectively than those of competitors further east. Finally, Rochester propagators enjoyed direct access to seedling imports, which "offered an escape from the diseases which were infecting some older nurseries," while the "slow-sailing vessels on the Atlantic protected the American market from easy exploitation by European horticulturists."[52] The roles of Rochester and Western New York in the rise of the national and international nursery trade and related agricultural improvement during the antebellum period provide many valuable insights about relationships among science, capitalism, and environmental history. Two exciting recent books expand upon McKelvey's foundational scholarship in this area: Emily Pawley's *The Nature of the Future: Agriculture, Science, and Capitalism in the Antebellum North* and Camden Burd's *The Roots of Flower City: Horticulture, Empire, and the Remaking of Rochester, New York.*[53]

In addition to embracing floriculture, mid-nineteenth-century Rochesterians sought to boost the growing manufacturing sector. Accordingly, a noteworthy socioenvironmental aspect of what McKelvey calls Rochester's movement "toward urban maturity" during the 1840s and 1850s was the rise of coal as a substitute for waterpower, or rather, a desired substitute.[54] Though Rochester's reputation as the "Young Lion of the West" receded as new western boomtowns emerged, its population surpassed 43,000 by 1855. Increasing numbers of residents and businesses sought to adopt the nation's new energy-intensive technologies, such as gas lighting, the telegraph, and factories for producing clothing, shoes, and other articles on an industrial scale; that is, powered by steam engines. Already straining to meet demand, the Genesee River flow diminished during droughts in 1851 and 1852, further compounding the sense of urgency about what we might now call the water-energy crisis of antebellum Rochester.

By concentrating vast amounts of energy, coal fueled the Industrial Revolution and provided a beacon for capitalist entrepreneurs. As McKelvey notes, the Erie Canal and other waterways conveyed cheap grades of coal from the Ohio River Valley to Rochester during the mid-1830s, and the first shipments of anthracite, the most energy-dense form of coal, arrived in 1851 from northeastern Pennsylvania via the emerging railroad system. While increased coal supplies enabled Flour City entrepreneurs to build new foundries, trip-hammer shops, and other manufacturing endeavors, overall, high coal prices precluded local inventors from getting a jump on their rivals elsewhere. As McKelvey puts it, "Rochester's industrial prospects were considerably embarrassed."[55]

Conclusion

The book ends rather abruptly, with an anecdote based on an essay published in one of the Rochester newspapers in 1855. The visiting author, who used the name "Gothamite," marveled at the city's failure to maximize the productivity of the Genesee River falls. But the visitor had been deceived by a spring flood. Had the Gothamite visited a few months later, when normal flow rates resumed, "he might have realized that Rochester's springtime had passed and that its future growth would depend upon an unfolding of its new human resources and other advantages, for the potentialities of the water-power era had been largely developed by the mid-fifties."[56] McKelvey leaves his readers there, awaiting his next volume, *Rochester: The Flower City, 1855–1890* (published in 1949), to pick up the story of Rochester's metaphorical summertime during the enormously transformative eras of the Civil War and the Gilded Age.

As I hope this essay has demonstrated, McKelvey's work continues to speak to environmentally oriented scholars and citizens today. While invoking some old-fashioned determinist approaches, the book remains insightful for those interested in the history of energy transitions, urban transformation and environmental disasters, and climate disruption and adaptation. McKelvey's book, as well as the primary sources upon which he relied, supplemented with other evidence and frameworks that have emerged since the 1940s, still have illustrative stories to tell about the evolution of relationships between people and the environment of the Flour and Flower Cities. Above all, *Rochester: The Water-Power City* remains a valuable reminder of the essential role played by water and other irreplaceable planetary resources in urban and human development.

Acknowledgments

I would like to thank Tamar Carroll, the *Rochester History* editorial team, and the RIT Humanities Writing Group for their excellent questions and suggestions. ▪

1. Terje Tvedt, *Water and Society: Changing Perceptions of Societal and Historical Development* (I.B. Tauris, 2021), https://library.oapen.org/handle/20.500.12657/58839, quote on xi.
2. Tvedt, *Water and Society*, 202.
3. See, for example, John R. McNeill, "The State of the Field of Environmental History," *Annual Review of Environment and Resources* 35 (2010): 345–74; Paul S. Sutter, "The World with Us: The State of American Environmental History," *Journal of American History* 100 (2013): 94–119.
4. For but a few illustrative examples, see Donald Worster, *Rivers of Empire: Water, Aridity, and the Growth of the American West* (Pantheon Books, 1985); Richard White, *The Organic Machine: The Remaking of the Columbia River* (Hill and Wang, 1995); Matthew Morse Booker, *Down by the Bay: San Francisco's History between the Tides* (University of California Press, 2013); Helen M. Rozwadowski, "The Promise of Ocean History for Environmental History," *Journal of American History* 100 (2013): 136–39; Steve Mentz, *An Introduction to the Blue Humanities* (Routledge, 2024); Daniel Macfarlane, *The Lives of Lake Ontario: An Environmental History* (McGill-Queen's Press, 2024); Ellen F. Arnold, *Water in World History* (Routledge, 2024).
5. Christof Mauch and Thomas G. Zeller, eds., "Rivers in History and Historiography: An Introduction," *Rivers in History: Perspectives on Waterways in Europe and North America* (University of Pittsburgh Press, 2008), 2.
6. See, for example, "What is Social History?" *History Today* 35, no. 3 (1985), https://www.historytoday.com/archive/what-social-history.
7. Michael Brown, "The Completists: Blake McKelvey, Bessie Louise Pierce, and Urban Biography," *Rochester History* 83, no. 1 (2025): 37–60; Bessie Louise Pierce, *A History of Chicago, Volume 1: The Beginning of a City, 1673–1848* (University of Chicago Press, 1937, reprinted 2007).
8. Dexter Perkins, Preface, *Rochester: The Water-Power City, 1812–1854* (Harvard University Press, 1945), v.
9. Perkins, Preface, *Rochester*, vi.
10. Arthur M. Schlesinger, "The City in American History," *Mississippi Valley Historical Review* 27 (1940): 43–66.
11. On the rise of urban environmental history, see Martin V. Melosi, "The Place of the City in Environmental History," *Environmental History Review* 17 (1993): 1–23; Christine

Meisner Rosen and Joel Arthur Tarr, "The Importance of an Urban Perspective in Environmental History," *Journal of Urban History* 20 (1994): 299–310. On the emergence of urban river studies, see Mauch and Zeller, *Rivers in History*; Stéphane Castonguay and Matthew Evenden, eds., *Urban Rivers: Remaking Rivers, Cities, and Space in Europe and North America* (University of Pittsburgh Press, 2012); Jason M. Kelly, Philip Scarpino, Helen Berry, James Syvitski, and Michael Meybeck, eds., *Rivers of the Anthropocene* (University of California Press, 2017); Matthew Evenden, "Beyond the Organic Machine? New Approaches in River Historiography," *Environmental History* 23 (2018): 698–720; Etienne Benson, "Rivers in History: Systems, Agents, and Places," in Elena Aronova, David Sepkoski, and Marco Tamborini, eds., *Handbook of the Historiography of the Earth and Environmental Sciences: Historiographies of Science* (Spinger Cham, 2024): 1–17, https://doi.org/10.1007/978-3-030-92679-3_12-1.

12. Rosen and Tarr, "The Importance of an Urban Perspective," quotes on 307 and 301, respectively.

13. Blake McKelvey, *Rochester: The Water-Power City, 1812-1854* (Harvard University Press, 1945), 3.

14. McKelvey, *Rochester*, 6, 5, 7.

15. See, for example, Simon Donner, "The Ugly History of Climate Determinism is Still Evident Today," *Scientific American*, June 24, 2020, https://www.scientificamerican.com/article/the-ugly-history-of-climate-determinism-is-still-evident-today/.

16. McKelvey, *Rochester*, 7.

17. See, for example, Eric E. Jones and James W. Wood, "Using Event-History Analysis to Examine the Causes of Semi-Sedentism among Shifting Cultivators: A Case Study of the Haudenosaunee, AD 1500-1700," *Journal of Archaeological Science* 39 (2012): 2593–603; Jennifer Birch, "Current Research on the Historical Development of Northern Iroquoian Societies," *Journal of Archaeological Research* 23 (2015): 263–323.

18. McKelvey, *Rochester*, 29, 36, 41.

19. Brown, "The Completists," 43.

20. McKelvey, *Rochester*, 54.

21. See, for example, Richard B. Stothers, "The Great Tambora Eruption in 1815 and Its Aftermath," *Science* 224 (1984): 1191–98; John D. Post, *The Last Great Subsistence Crisis in the Western World* (Johns Hopkins University Press, 1977); Gillen D'Arcy Wood, *Tambora: The Eruption that Changed the World* (Princeton University Press, 2014).

22. McKelvey, *Rochester*, 65.

23. McKelvey, *Rochester*, 91.

24. McKelvey, *Rochester*, 65.

25. McKelvey, *Rochester*, 71.

26. McKelvey, *Rochester*, 71, 119.

27. McKelvey, *Rochester*, 187.

28. McKelvey, *Rochester*, 304, 355.

29. Rebecca Rafferty, "RMSC's Resurrection Role," *City Newspaper*, July 1, 2015, https://www.roccitymag.com/arts-entertainment/rmscs-resurrection-role-2574182.

30. McKelvey did write a book on this topic much later in his career, but many opportunities remain for expanding historical scholarship about the snowbelt of the Great Lakes and northeastern North America. Blake McKelvey, *Snow in the Cities: A History of America's Urban Response* (University of Rochester Press, 1995); Mark Monmonier, *Lake Effect: Tales of Large Lakes, Arctic Winds, and Recurrent Snows* (Syracuse University Press, 2012); Timothy W. Kneeland, *Declaring Disaster: Buffalo's Blizzard of '77 and the Creation of FEMA* (Syracuse University Press, 2021).

31. McKelvey, *Rochester*, 83.

32. McKelvey, *Rochester*, 72.

33. McKelvey, *Rochester*, 163.

34. McKelvey, *Rochester*, 99.

35. McKelvey, *Rochester*, 299.

36. McKelvey, *Rochester*, 110, 116, 178.

37. McKelvey, *Rochester*, 249, 251.

38. McKelvey, *Rochester*, 337n71.

39. See, for example, Gareth Davies, "Dealing with Disaster: The Politics of Catastrophe in the United States, 1789-1861," *American Nineteenth Century History* 14 (2013): 53-72.

40. McKelvey, *Rochester*, 180-81.

41. McKelvey, *Rochester*, 257.

42. McKelvey, *Rochester*, 257-58.

43. McKelvey, *Rochester*, 339.

44. See, for example, Dorceta E. Taylor, *The Environment and the People in American Cities, 1600s-1900s: Disorder, Inequality, and Social Change* (Duke University Press, 2009).

45. McKelvey, *Rochester*, 340.

46. *Report on Cholera*, 39-41, quoted in McKelvey, *Rochester*, 341.

47. See, for example, Steven Johnson, *The Ghost Map: The Story of London's Most Terrifying Epidemic—and How it Changed Science, Cities, and the Modern World* (Riverhead Books, 2006).

48. McKelvey, *Rochester*, 342.

49. Rosser H. Taylor, "The Sale and Application of Commercial Fertilizers in the South Atlantic States to 1900," *Agricultural History* 21 (1947): 46-52.

50. McKelvey, *Rochester*, 238.

51. McKelvey, *Rochester*, 239.

52. McKelvey, *Rochester*, 239.

53. Emily Pawley, *The Nature of the Future: Agriculture, Science, and Capitalism in the Antebellum North* (University of Chicago Press, 2020); Camden Burd, *The Roots of Flower City: Horticulture, Empire, and the Remaking of Rochester, New York* (Cornell University Press, 2024).

54. McKelvey, *Rochester*, 322.

55. McKelvey, *Rochester*, 327.

56. McKelvey, *Rochester*, 365.

"Faithfully Thought Out: The Artistic Collaborations of M. Louise Stowell and Harvey Ellis"

Memorial Art Gallery, Rochester, NY, June 28, 2024–January 5, 2025.

Faithfully Thought Out and Patiently Evolved: The Work of M. Louise Stowell and Harvey Ellis

Kerry Schauber and Lauren Tagliaferro, eds. Rochester, NY: RIT Press, 2024.

Sarah Thompson

The exhibition and book *Faithfully Thought Out* together restore the legacy of a Rochester artist, explore the complicated nature of collaborative work, and present a fascinating image of turn-of-the-century Rochester's connections to modern art movements. Both the show and the related publication focus on the relationship between M. Louise Stowell (1861–1930) and Harvey Ellis (1852–1904), colleagues and friends who maintained side-by-side studios in the Powers Building on Main Street in downtown Rochester. Stowell, whose family moved to Rochester in 1863, was a student in the newly established Fine Arts program at the Mechanics Institute (now Rochester Institute of Technology) in the late 1880s; she went on to teach at the Institute for several years before studying at a summer art school outside Boston, then in New York City at the Metropolitan Museum of Art's art school and at the Art Students League. She subsequently returned to Rochester for the remainder of her career.

Ellis was born in Rochester, attended and was dismissed from West Point, and then joined his older brother's architectural firm, although relatively little is known about any formal training he may have had in the arts. After his brother was charged with bribery, Ellis left the city to work in various architectural offices across the Midwest, eventually resuming his place in his brother's practice in Rochester in 1894. Between 1894 and mid-1903, Stowell and Ellis's professional and social connections multiplied: Not only did they occupy neighboring studios, but they cofounded the Rochester Arts

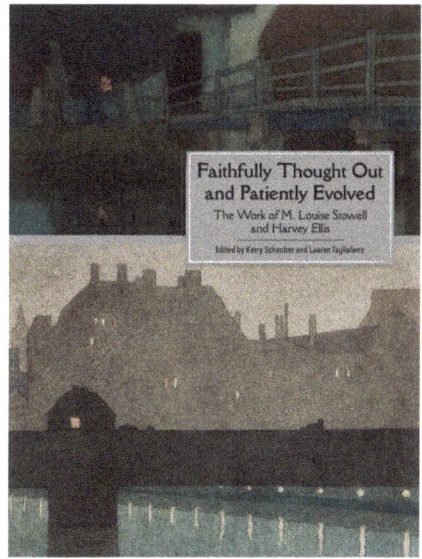

and Crafts Society in 1897; periodically taught at the Mechanics Institute; had an overlapping circle of friends, including architect Claude Bragdon and his sister, May Bragdon; and, most importantly, worked with shared inspirations and techniques, resulting in intersecting bodies of work. Following Ellis's death and Stowell's retreat from artmaking due to poor health, her reputation diminished. To prior generations, Stowell—younger and a woman—might be reduced to playing the role of muse for Ellis, but the show and catalog reject this stereotypical narrative to establish the breadth of her work and their shared inspirations, demonstrating her agency as an artist and educator.

The title of both the exhibition and the accompanying publication quote from a pedagogical publication by Stowell, who advocated for the necessity of careful, studied artistic production. In the small space of the Rochester Memorial Art Gallery's Lockhart Gallery, "Faithfully Thought Out: The Artistic Collaborations of M. Louise Stowell and Harvey Ellis" offered proof of this conscientious labor—presenting a compelling, though by necessity selective, overview of Stowell's and Ellis's shared interests and artistic practices and documenting their mutually influential and iterative output of drawings, watercolors, and prints. While both artists were based in Rochester for significant portions of their careers, their work reflects their participation in international trends: the Arts and Crafts movement, placing them in the company of Western New York practitioners like Gustav Stickley and Elbert Hubbard, as well as the Aesthetic movement, Art Nouveau, the Pictorialist movement in photography, the fascination with Japanese prints, and the growing circulation of illustrated print media.

Curating a show in a small space like the Lockhart Gallery is a challenge, particularly given the breadth of possibilities for inclusion: Stowell's and Ellis's art, with subject matter spanning literary illustrations, historic settings, allegorical scenes, landscapes, rural labor, city views, and contemporary advertising; supporting materials from their archives; and comparative works that illustrate their relationships with multiple artistic movements. In fact, the show made use of space beyond the gallery: Five watercolors by the artists were showcased on the external wall leading to the entry, enticing the visitor with a preview of the show's content. Stowell's *Mill by the Falls* displays watercolor techniques used by both artists—washes of color, dominated by teals, blues, grays, and sepia tones—applied over a charcoal base, resulting in a velvety, saturated finish, with contours delineated by thin lines of black ink. The painting looks like a print, an effect heightened by the application of deep blue at the top of the scene. The wall text notes that both the blue and the composition, which uses a flattening high angle to present mill buildings over turbulent waters and cuts off the scene at the left side, reflect the influence of the Japanese woodblock prints that Stowell collected. Artists of multiple late nineteenth-century movements—Impressionism, Post-Impressionism, Arts and Crafts, Aestheticism, Art Nouveau—were intrigued by Japanese prints, which used color, line, and composition in distinctly different ways than European academic training would allow. Stowell shared that interest, inspiring her to reimagine the familiar surroundings of Rochester as if it were Tokyo during the Edo period.

Placing these images outside the gallery gave the visitor the opportunity to study them individually, although also

Views of "Faithfully
Thought Out:
The Artistic
Collaborations of
M. Louise Stowell
and Harvey Ellis"
as installed in the
Lockhart Gallery at
the Memorial Art
Gallery, Rochester,
fall 2024. *Photo
by Andy Olenick/
Fotoworks.*

isolating them from the rest of the show, where strategic groupings and supporting archival materials contextualized Stowell's and Ellis's careers. Within the Lockhart Gallery, the curators used the limited space, as well as the challenges of works on paper—modest in scale, subject to fading, and prone to damage over time—to their advantage. The size of the works and their muted palettes require close study, but the arrangement within the confines of the gallery space created a sense of intimacy and quiet rather than seeming overcrowded. The show included examples of sketches, source materials, and finished works to illustrate the artists' inspirations and the entwined nature of their production and highlighted their use of shared models, motifs, color palettes, and techniques in the wall arrangements. Stowell's *Young Timothy Learned Sin to Flee* and Ellis's *Sin* were placed side by side, and although neither is dated, making it difficult to determine who originated the motif, both use a recognizably similar female figure with Medusa-like hair. Ellis's *Port Scene* used an image of the Buffalo Sand Company from Stowell's scrapbook collection as a source; one of the scrapbook volumes, filled with cyanotypes, was on view in the show. Ellis's *The Hour Glass* was based on a photograph of a posed Stowell, also included in the show. Stowell used photographs of herself as references in her own work as well, exemplified by the inclusion of her study and watercolor *Philosophia*. An ink-and-wash drawing found among Ellis's papers, *Landscape with a Reclining Woman*, was shown next to a closely matching drawing from Stowell's sketchbook, posing questions about how to unravel their connection: Did Stowell create both, and *Landscape* has been mistaken for Ellis's work because it ended up in his

papers? Was one inspired directly by, or even traced from, the other? As the label suggested, could this be a kind of game of transformation between the artists, with the ink-and-wash version highlighting the optical illusion of a landscape shifting to a prone woman's form?

Each theme in the show reiterated the artists' mutable connections. Stowell designed innovative posters, aligning her with Art Nouveau developments in Europe and with the rise of color printing in advertising. Her lithograph *George P. Humphrey at the Sign of the "Old Book Man,"* circa 1895, a poster advertising a bookseller based at 25 Exchange Street, shows a seated man reading, a cropped figure descending the stairs to his left. The flattened composition, with a sharp foreground and background contrast, reflects her Japanese interests, while the linear geometry and letter forms connect her to the latest Art Nouveau design. Her *Third National Cycle Exhibition* poster earned an honorable mention in a German competition; the wall label noted that it was formerly attributed to Ellis, although contemporary news stories clarify that it was made by Stowell. Both artists created illustration cycles, and Stowell's biblical illustrations for *The New England Primer* were included, as were Ellis's study and watercolor of a scene from *The Odyssey*. Stowell had a woodblock of Ellis's *Odyssey* illustration produced, and had it printed in Japan after Ellis's death. Medievalism influenced both artists, as was the case for many involved in the Arts and Crafts movement. They sometimes adapted sources from print media for inspiration, as with Ellis's *Sortie from the Castle*, with a setting inspired by an architectural journal's illustration of a medieval gatehouse. The curators placed Stowell's and Ellis's drawings of medieval interior scenes—seemingly inspired by the same source—one above the other; the accompanying wall label suggested that the attribution of the drawings may have been mistakenly switched, as Ellis's architectural training would make him more likely to be the creator of the drawing credited to Stowell. In the absence of documentation of how either artist would describe their creative interactions, the nature of their artistic relationship is ultimately unresolved, but the curators used the selections in the show to highlight intricate crossovers in their practices that suggest nuanced cooperation between peers.

It is somewhat unusual for an exhibition at the Memorial Art Gallery to be accompanied by a publication, merited in this circumstance by MAG's recent acquisitions, the artists' local ties, and the opportunity to present new research illuminating their careers. *Faithfully Thought Out and Patiently Evolved: The Work of M. Louise Stowell and Harvey Ellis* is edited by the show's curators, but it is not a traditional catalog in that it doesn't record the specific works selected for the show or preserve their arrangement. The volume includes an introduction followed by three interpretive essays, with most of the pages given to reproducing Stowell's and then Ellis's work much more prolifically than would have been possible in the gallery space. The essays occupy the first third of the book, and organization then sacrifices the thoughtful groupings from the exhibition in favor of presenting each artist separately: A selection of Stowell's work comprises the next third of the book, and Ellis's work fills the last. Their art can thus be considered distinctly, within the span of their respective careers, but at the expense of the exhibition's and essays' emphasis on Stowell's and Ellis's complex relationship. Where possible, studies and

sketches are placed alongside finished works, leading the reader through steps in the process of making and illustrating Stowell's titular quote. The matte finish of the catalog complements the muted colors and saturation of the artists' works on paper.

Kerry Schauber's introduction provides immediate context for the show: In 2016, the Memorial Art Gallery acquired a large collection of Stowell's and Ellis's works formerly held by the Strong National Museum of Play. At the same time, the University of Rochester's River Campus Libraries received archival materials related to Stowell and Ellis from the Strong. The Memorial Art Gallery thus had an opportunity to examine the careers of significant local artists whose work was relatively little known to the public. Schauber emphasizes that the show and catalog revive Stowell's reputation: more so than Ellis's, her career and contributions have been overlooked, and her career was, until recently, subsumed by his. Of the three essays that follow, Patricia Tice's "A High Order of Talent" establishes a biography of Stowell; Susan Futterman's "Kindred Spirits" focuses on the collaborative relationship between Stowell and Ellis in the context of their circle of friends; and Patricia D. Hamm's "M. Louise Stowell and Harvey Ellis: Characteristics of Their Artworks" provides a brief technical overview that supports the artists' close ties, noting the difficulties of telling their work apart due to their shared materials and techniques.

Given Stowell's near-disappearance from the history of art, Tice's biographical essay provides satisfying analysis of the connections between Stowell's Rochester home and the wider contemporary art world. Futterman's essay fills in additional details of Stowell's and Ellis's work between 1894 and 1903 and of Ellis's career, noting their shared friendships with architect and designer Claude Bragdon and his sister, May Bragdon. Two important themes connecting Stowell's and Ellis's shared career circumstances emerge in these essays. The first is the constant balance of proximity and distance in their training, influences, and artistic practices. Stowell trained and taught locally, as did Ellis, but both also traveled to larger cities and established networks far from home. Both showed work outside of Rochester, notably in Buffalo, Albany, Chicago, Philadelphia, and New York, and Stowell entered a German poster contest. Both balanced local, observational subject matter with scenes drawn from literature, religion, and a fantasized medieval past. Both appreciated Japanese art, with Stowell particularly known for her interest; she published on Japanese prints in Gustav Stickley's Arts and Crafts journal *The Craftsman*, and in her late career she would open an import shop. Tice notes that Stowell probably learned about Japanese art and printmaking by attending the lectures of Boston Museum of Fine Arts curator Ernest Fenollosa. Did Stowell's enthusiasm intensify Ellis's connection with *ukiyo-e*—literally, "pictures of the floating world"—woodblock prints of subjects associated with the entertainment district of Edo? Or had he already established this taste, perhaps through his own exploration of Arts and Crafts design? Considering the impact on their artistic directions, it would be helpful to explore this connection further with additional comparisons between Stowell's and Ellis's work and *ukiyo-e*.

The centrality of print media emerges as a second major theme, and it is the circulation of print media that largely bridged the local and national or international aspects of their careers. Not only did both artists work on paper, but the circulation of media on paper—vastly expanded by later nineteenth-century technological advances in printing (particularly color printing), photographic reproduction, and transportation—inspired them, drove their collecting habits, and allowed them to disseminate their work widely. Tice notes that Stowell's use of photography was not atypical of an artist of her era: Stowell kept scrapbooks filled with newspaper and magazine clippings, cyanotypes, and photographic prints, and both artists drew from the print materials from her scrapbooks for inspiration. The Japanese prints that intrigued both artists were affordable and available precisely because they were prints. Both artists had an appreciation for posters, and Claude Bragdon fed this interest when he shared new chromolithogaphic posters after returning from his European travels. The proliferation of affordable works on paper, and the speed at which they could travel, meant that Stowell and Ellis could collect and organize works that inspired them and that they could take part in contemporary developments from their homes in Rochester, both as consumers of print media and as authors and illustrators whose work was published in print. Modern technology thus allowed for participation in the modern art world from Rochester in ways that would simply not have been possible even a few decades earlier.

In both the show and the book, Stowell emerges as the more intriguing figure. Ellis's early career seems to draw on more predictable settings and subjects of the Realist movement—farmers and laborers in rural landscapes—or reflects his work in architecture and design, while Stowell experiments with more modern trends. Perhaps she was also more influential on

Ellis than vice versa: of the two, she was the one with the more expansive art education, and after all, her scrapbooks and her modeling provided their shared source material. Tice raises the issues of what has become of Stowell's work, as she has found published references to paintings by Stowell that have disappeared from circulation. Hopefully this will spark further investigation to reconstitute Stowell's career.

Speculating on the reasons for the losses again brings us back to the themes of the show: Perhaps Stowell's gender made her work more likely to be dismissed; perhaps being more known for works on paper resulted in an ephemeral legacy; perhaps the nature of her collaboration with Ellis means that some of her work is not lost but remains entangled with his. ■

A Symbiotic Partnership: Marrying Commerce to Education at Gustav Stickley's 1903 Arts and Crafts Exhibitions

by Bruce A. Austin. Rochester, NY: RIT Press, 2022.

Aspen Golann, Rhode Island School of Design and The Chairmaker's Toolbox

A Symbiotic Partnership: Marrying Commerce to Education at Gustav Stickley's 1903 Arts & Crafts Exhibitions by Bruce A. Austin provides a meticulous examination of a pivotal moment in design and craft history. The book delves deep into the intricacies of Gustav Stickley's influential 1903 exhibition, held in Syracuse before traveling on to Rochester. Austin's examination of the events of 1903 offers valuable insights into a unique intersection between art and commerce and into the intertwined roles of salesmanship and academic institutions during a transformative period for both design and commerce.

A scholar who specialized in American decorative arts and the Arts and Crafts movement, Austin brings a wealth of expertise to his exploration of Stickley's exhibitions. *A Symbiotic Partnership* was penned in 2022, marking a recent addition to the scholarship on Stickley and the conventions of craft commerce in the early twentieth century. Through a detailed analysis of historical documents and archival materials, Austin demonstrates how Stickley leveraged his exhibitions to cultivate relationships with educators, students, and consumers alike, thereby helping shape the trajectory of craft-marketing strategies and American design education.

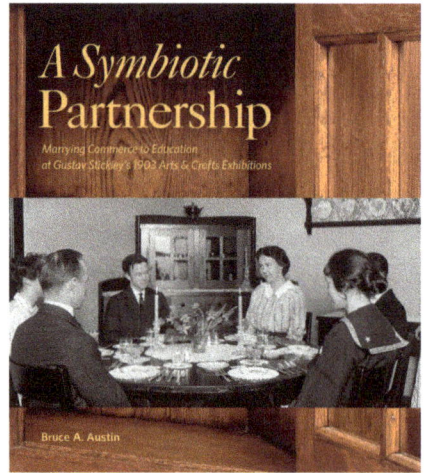

In Rochester, the exhibition of Arts and Crafts designers, anchored by Gustav Stickley, coincided with the two-year anniversary of the opening of the Eastman Building at the Mechanic's Institute (now Rochester Institute of Technology). It was supported by the Rochester Arts and Crafts Society, the oldest such society in the country. The society had gained a new member, Theodore Hanford Pond, when he was hired in 1902 by the Department of Applied and Fine Arts at the institute. Interestingly, he was hired away from the Department of Design and Applied Art at the Rhode Island School of Design. It was most likely Pond who was instrumental in arranging for Stickley's exhibition to travel from Syracuse to Rochester, the first time a design exhibition of this sort had traveled between venues.

In the landscape of existing scholarship, Austin's work occupies a unique niche. The central argument of the book revolves around Stickley's approach to publicity and its relationship to the incitement of a design movement. Austin contends that these exhibitions served as more than mere showcases for furniture—they represented a partnership between Stickley and educational institutions. Through this partnership, Stickley's work gained an implied sense of academic and cultural value from association with the Mechanics Institute, and, in turn, the Mechanics Institute elevated its position in art and design education by serving as an academic champion of the Arts and Crafts movement and the design scene.

Austin's writing style is scholarly and thoroughly researched, and while the subject matter is highly specific, readers are ultimately rewarded with a nuanced understanding of this pivotal moment in the history of design and commerce.

Austin's methodology is rigorous and methodical. The depth of his evidence is compelling as he draws on a wide array of primary sources—including photographs, correspondence, exhibition catalogs, and contemporary accounts—to reconstruct the intricate web of relationships that characterized Stickley's world. Austin's adept use of evidence lends credibility to his narrative, enabling readers to grasp both the complexities of the 1903 exhibitions and their significance within the broader context of American design history.

A Symbiotic Partnership: Marrying Commerce to Education at Gustav Stickley's 1903 Arts and Crafts Exhibitions provides a comprehensive exploration of a specific moment in design history while addressing broader societal shifts and ideological tensions surrounding craftsmanship, mass production, and consumerism. Bruce A. Austin's meticulous research and nuanced analysis offer valuable contributions to our understanding of this transformative period, making this book a worthwhile read for scholars, students, and enthusiasts alike. ◾

The Crucible of Public Policy: New York Courts in the Progressive Era

by Bruce W. Dearstyne. Albany, NY: SUNY Press, 2022.

Hon. Richard A. Dollinger, Ret.

Rochester, New York, is the birthplace of America's right to privacy.

That's the conclusion of author and historian Bruce W. Dearstyne in his 2022 book *The Crucible of Public Policy, New York Courts in the Progressive Era*. The book highlights the decisions of the New York Court of Appeals, the state's highest court. It focuses on the cultural moment when the explosive growth of technology and mass marketing consumerism at the end of the nineteenth century sparked new challenges for the emerging working and middle classes in the early years of the twentieth century.

Dearstyne's book encompasses nearly three decades of court decisions that charted the new progressive direction for New York and the rest of the nation. The Court of Appeals, the most prominent court in the country, vied with the United States Supreme Court to be the final voice on legislative efforts to control working conditions for families and children in a booming industrial age.

The book is laden with legal arguments; its detailed analyses of various legal briefs might prove a challenge for nonlawyers. However, the book opens with a clear and gripping case: that of a Rochester teenager who claimed she owned her image. The technologies that permitted both the capture and the exploitation of her image have a Rochester focus.

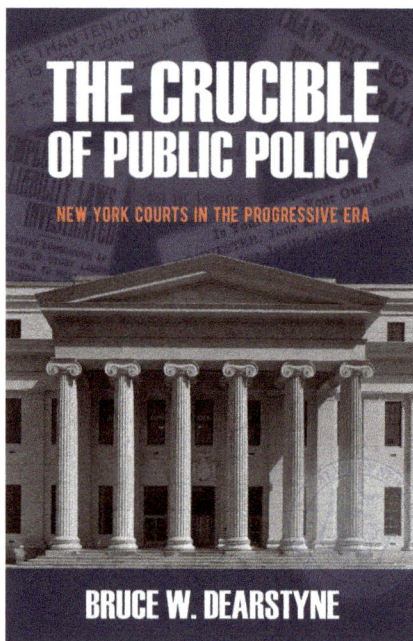

George Eastman premiered the easy-to-use Kodak camera in 1888, and personal photography soon swept the nation. Almost simultaneously, halftone printing emerged, allowing photographs to be transferred into newspapers and other print media. Suddenly, images of both ordinary and prominent Americans appeared in wider circulation in newspapers and magazines.

The circulation of such photographs in print captivated the nation. To the rising and now literate middle classes, pictures were worth at least a thousand words. Even Mark Twain remarked: "I don't care much about reading but I do like to look at pictures." Theodore Roosevelt complained about prying cameras that wanted "to Kodak him."

Advertisers, seeking to entice emerging middle-class consumers, discovered the power of using feminine portraits to lure consumers to their products.

Abigail Roberson, a teenager who lived in Rochester's Corn Hill neighborhood, discovered that her portrait— perhaps purloined by a jilted boyfriend—had been widely circulated on boxes of flour by the Rochester Folding Box Company to promote "Flour of the Family," a product of Franklin Mills. After she learned of the image, Roberson, who never consented and was never consulted beforehand, suffered nervous shock. She was confined to bed and was ridiculed by friends who recognized her face.

Her family commenced an action for wrongful appropriation of her image here in Monroe County Supreme Court, under a new doctrine advanced by two Boston legal scholars, Louis Brandeis and Samuel Warren. Their *Harvard Law Review* article—"The Right to Privacy"—argued that the new photograph and print technologies "invaded the sacred precincts of private and domestic life" and impinged on an individual's private right to be left alone.

In August 1900, the court in Rochester agreed, holding that any modest person whose likeness was used without permission would be shocked and wounded to find their "right of privacy violated." If Roberson's image as a young woman had value in the commercial world, then the right to that value belonged to her. Ms. Roberson sought $15,000 in damages, which would be $450,000 in today's currency. The Appellate Division Fourth

Department affirmed, leaving the matter up to the Court of Appeals.

Dearstyne artfully sets up the debate for the new privacy concept before the state's highest court. The Chief Judge at the time was Alton B. Parker, a Democrat in a state that was largely controlled by Republicans, including, in 1900, by the ultimate Progressive—but camera shy—Republican, Theodore Roosevelt.

Parker, while sitting on the bench, had loftier ambitions, which would eventually lead to his becoming the Democratic candidate for president in 1904 against fellow New Yorker Roosevelt. However, Parker's ambitions did not extend to recognizing Abigail Roberson's right to control her own image. He passed on the opportunity to create new law. Instead, in a long and what can under today's standards only be considered a condescending and sexist opinion, Parker, leading a 4–3 majority, held in June 1902 that Roberson's image— her face—had no inherent value. Further, Roberson had suffered no physical harm. In fact, Parker suggested that, in his view, the use of her image was a compliment to her beauty. Any creation of a right to privacy was left to the state legislature, not the courts, the majority intoned.

As Dearstyne notes, the three dissenting judges strongly disagreed, arguing that Roberson's injuries, such as the wounds to her feelings and being subject to social ridicule or contempt, were real, irreparable, and compensable. Cultural critics of the court, too, abounded. *The New York Times* even suggested that, had the injured plaintiff been Parker's daughter, the decision would have been quite different.

Importantly, as Dearstyne highlights, the state Legislature did take up Judge Parker's invitation. Within three years, New York State enacted the first-in-the-nation privacy protection law, which is now Sections 50 and 51 of the state's Civil Rights Law.

Roberson, denied her claim by Judge Parker, may have had the last word. During the 1904 presidential campaign, Parker objected to press photographers stalking his home, including as he emerged from his daily swim in the Hudson River.

Roberson wrote a letter to *The New York Times*, which published it on the front page. She chastised the candidate for seeking a right to control his image when he had denied the very same right to her.

She was a "poor girl making my living by my daily efforts" while he was a vaunted presidential candidate. She concluded, "The right you denied me but which you now assert for yourself was stronger in my case than yours."

This book is a window into the fierce debate over the right to privacy as it was waged before the rise of television, the internet, or social media. It reminds us that balancing individual privacy rights in an ever-increasingly technologically diverse world remains a challenge with us and for us still. ▪

www.ingramcontent.com/pod-product-compliance
Lightning Source LLC
Chambersburg PA
CBHW042349040426

42448CB00019B/3477